BOEING B-52G/H STRATOFORTRESS STORY

B-52H, 60-0053, of the 7th BW as seen from the boom operator's position in a KC-135. The Strategic Camouflage scheme appears in this April 2, 1987 photo. "0053" is modified for ALCM carriage as is visible by the non-functional ALT-32 antennae on the aft fuselage sides. Note the slightly extended spoilers on the left wing.

CREDITS:

The authors and **Aerofax Inc.** would like to thank the following individuals for their assistance in assembling the reference materials and photographic images necessary for the successful completion of this book: Jake Babbitt; Dave Beesley; Jim Benson; Michael S. Binder; Joe Bruch; James Burridge; Maj. Barbara Carr; George Cockle; Col. Peyton Cole; Tom Cole, Boeing; Peter Dakin, Boeing; David Dison, Boeing; Col. Tom Ellers; Kelly Green; Wesley B. Henry, Air Force Museum; Robert Hopkins; Sgt. Marc Hughes; Col. Mike Kehoe; Jon Kersten (SAC/LGMSD); John C. Kidwell; Grant Larkins, Boeing; 2nd Lt. Nori LaRue-Musgrave; Gayle Lawson; Don Logan; John W. McCarty, Westinghouse; Don McGarry; Larry Milberry; Susan Miller; Paul Minert; Matt Oswald; Terry Panopalis; LtC. George Peck (SAC/PA); LtC. Paul Pederson; Bill Plemmons; Paul Ragusa; Maj. Eric Reffett; Mick Roth; Col. John Sams; Doug Slowiak; LtC. Andy Smoak; Eva Smoke; Bob Snellenberg, Boeing; Mike Wagnon; Barbara Wasson; Michael White; Tom Williams, McDonnell Douglas Space Systems Co.; and Col. Dave Young.

PROGRAM HISTORY:

Boeing Military Airplane Company's model 464 series, known more commonly under the formal military designation B-52, stands tall as the unquestioned high-water mark of U.S. strategic deterrent forces in the post-WWII period. Tagged with the official name of *Stratofortress*[1], crewmembers more generally refer to it as the "BUFF", meaning "Big Ugly Fat Fellow".

BACKGROUND

During January 1946 the Air Materiel Command issued requirements for a heavy bomber to replace the Convair B-36 then entering testing. The requirements called for an intercontinental aircraft with a top speed of 450 mph at 35,000 ft. and an operating radius of 5,000 miles with 10,000 lbs. of bombs. As the result of the ensuing design competition, Boeing was awarded a "phase 1" engineering study and preliminary design contract during June 1946.

Boeing's initial proposal was its model 462 with a 221 ft. wingspan. It generally resembled an enlarged B-29 powered by six Wright T-35 turboprop engines, and except for a slight range deficiency, met the desired requirements. However, this was a period of rapid technological advancement, and the model 462 quickly evolved into the model 464-29 with six more powerful Wright T-35-W-1 turboprops. The resulting changes enabled the aircraft to meet the desired range specification, but both the designers and the Air Force[2] desired more speed and higher cruising altitudes.

[2] Although the initial customer was the Army Air Forces (AAF), the U.S. Air Force (USAF) was created as a separate service before the B-52G/H reached production. Therefore, for the purposes of this publication, both the AAF and the USAF will be treated as the same entity.

Improved engine performance and the possibilities presented by aerial refueling entered the scene during 1947, and Boeing responded with an improved model 464-35 during January 1948. This proposal utilized four Wright T35-W-3 turboprops driving counter-rotating 19-ft. diameter propellers, but was somewhat smaller and faster than the model 464-29 and had a still longer range. The AF approved this design and issued a Phase 2 contract for the construction of a full-scale engineering mockup and two flyable experimental bomber aircraft. Work on this design moved forward quickly until it became obvious that the proposed engine and propeller would not materialize in the desired time frame. Regardless, the first public announcement of the new XB-52 was made on September 30, 1947.

Work on a turbojet-powered version of the model 464 began during the summer of 1948. This was the model 464-40, basically a model 464-35 powered by eight Westinghouse XJ40-WE-40 turbojet engines. The problems with the Wright turboprops and propellers was

The first B-52G, 57-6468, at rollout at the Boeing Wichita plant. The aircraft was in bare metal finish with dayglo orange panels on the fuselage sides and vertical fin. Underside was gloss white.

[1] In a continuing Boeing policy of including the word "Fortress" in the names of its long line of heavy bombers, and the word "Strato" in its pressurized, high-altitude, aircraft.

B-52G, 57-6468, later in its career while assigned to the 42d BW, Loring AFB, Maine. Weathering of the SIOP camouflage paint is typical.

B-52G, 57-6468, in the Strategic scheme at Mather AFB, 6 November 1987. Nose radome and EVS turrets have been removed for maintenance after a bird strike.

B-52G-75-BW, 57-6471, with photo target marking on spine for test activity. Other markings are standard for type and period.

JB-52G, 57-6471, fitted with TF33-P-3 engines, served as prototype B-52H. Fuselage had dayglo orange panels. J57s were later refitted. It's now ALCM capable.

becoming acute, and Boeing was advised that Pratt & Whitney (P&W) had started development of a powerful new turbojet, the J57. The marriage of the J57 to the 464-40 design yielded promising results in studies and the turboprop version was subsequently dropped during October 1948. The program continued with the pure-jet model 464-49 which utilized eight J57 engines and a swept wing derived from that used on the new Boeing B-47 medium bomber. The model 464-49 evolved into the model 464-67 as the design matured and this would be the definitive B-52 design as exhibited by the XB-52. Work on the two experimental aircraft continued, and it was subsequently decided to use the second aircraft as the service test example, hence it was redesignated YB-52.

The XB-52 (49-230) rolled out of Boeing's Seattle plant on November 29, 1951 and was moved into a large hanger for ground testing prior to its maiden flight. During a pneumatic system test the aircraft suffered extensive damage to the trailing edge of the wing and required major repairs. Meanwhile, the YB-52 (49-231) was rolled out on March 15 and made the first B-52 flight on April 15, 1952.[3]

Development of the first-generation *Stratofortress* configuration, which included the B-52A/B/C/D/E and F models (to be covered in a separate **Aerofax** monograph) eventually resulted in the production of 449 aircraft. These *Stratofortresses*, under the aegis of the Strategic Air Command (SAC), made what many military strategists consider the most important single element of the world's greatest aerial combat force.

[3] The XB-52 eventually made its first flight on October 15, 1952.

During the mid-1950s, and concurrent with the introduction of the B-52 into the operational inventory, the AF was in the middle of a debate over whether to move ahead with an expensive, and technologically unproven, program calling for the development of a supersonic, intercontinental, medium bomber. This precedent-setting project eventually gave birth to Convair's B-58 *Hustler* (see **Aerofax** *Aerograph 4, Convair B-58*), but not before the AF and the manufacturer were forced to maneuver though a very lengthy and near-disastrous development effort that cost several hundred million dollars and resulted in the production of only 116 aircraft.

"Super B-52"

Almost totally as a result of the B-58's then-tenuous future, Boeing began accelerating work on a long-standing in-house program to develop what then was referred to as the "super B-52". Because of the continuing set-backs with the B-58, the AF, and particularly SAC, had begun to conclude that the failure to seriously consider the development and production of a less technically advanced bomber might lead to an obsolescence of the U.S. strategic bomber force in the early-1960s before the B-58 could become operational.

By early-1955, the in-house studies at Boeing had already generated a number of possible upgrades to the basic B-52 configuration that would improve virtually every aspect of the aircraft's combat capability. As envisioned during late-May 1955, the new aircraft would include a B-52 fuselage with a redesigned wing and non-afterburning versions of the powerful P&W J75 turbojet engine which was scheduled to power the Republic F-105 and Convair F-106 fighters. This engine, designated JT4A in civil applications, generated approximately 16,000 lbs. thrust—nearly 5,000 lbs. more per engine that the production B-52's standard J57s. This additional thrust, at the expense of some additional weight, would give the aircraft considerably more performance and permit significantly higher gross takeoff weights.

Reaction to the "super B-52" initially proved lukewarm, due primarily to Gen. Curtis LeMay's (Commander-in-Chief, SAC) concerns over disrupting the first-generation B-52 production program. Because of this, initial funding, amounting to only $1.2 million for preliminary design studies, was delayed and Boeing therefore did not formally undertake work on the new model 464-253 until June 1956. Shortly thereafter, the Air Staff committed an additional $8.8 million to the project in order to review Boeing's proposed engineering changes.

Around the same time, the AF began searching for an advanced bomber to eventually replace the B-52 in the 1965-1975 period, issuing requirements for Weapon Systems 110A and 125A. WS-110A was to be a "subsonic cruise-supersonic dash" bomber, powered by turbojet engines burning a boron-based chemical "zip" fuel instead of conventional JP-3/4. WS-125A was to be an ultra-long range, supersonic-cruise, aircraft powered by nuclear engines then under development. The competitors for these proposed weapon systems narrowed to North American and Boeing for WS-110A and Convair for WS-125A. It appeared at this time that the B-52 would indeed be replaced by one or both of these proposed aircraft.

While Boeing investigated their WS-110A proposal, it forged ahead with trying to sell the "super B-52" as an interim missile launching platform. Boeing informally presented the model 464-253 to the Air Research and Development Command during March 1956. July saw Boeing hold an initial development engineering inspection at their Seattle production facility, this being used to determine the crew arrangement for what was becoming a considerable redesign of the original layout.

B-52G

On August 15, 1956, Boeing formally submitted a comprehensive B-52 model improvement program in response to questions posed by the AF at earlier, preliminary meetings. The Air Staff approved this plan on August 29, though stipulating that Boeing's effort should be on a "minimal sustaining basis" pending a decision concerning the future of the B-58 and WS-110A programs, as well as the ever-escalating AF budgetary constraints.

Boeing's model 464-253, now being referred to tentatively by the AF as the B-52G, was the first product of a data base that was generated around the operational experiences of the first-generation B-52s. Major improvements to the second-generation B-52 design included:

B-52G, 57-6509, of the 97th BW undergoes cold weather climatic testing at the McKinley climatic laboratory at Eglin AFB, Florida.

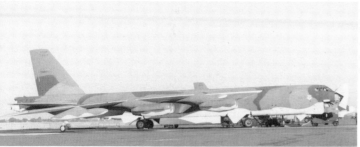
B-52G, 57-6512, of the 97th BW visits Castle AFB on June 26, 1984. Open nose radome shows location of ground mapping radar (lower) and ECM components (upper).

B-52G, 57-6514, in flight, in standard, but weathered, SIOP camouflage scheme. Aircraft has the AFSATCOM dome forward but lacks the ALQ-153 antenna on fin.

ALCM-modified B-52G, 58-0165, of the 319th BW at Grand Forks AFB, N. Dak. Wrap-around nose camouflage was a 1984 expedient to "tone down" white noses.

ALCM B-52G, 58-0177, of the 416th BW, transient at Castle AFB on August 28, 1984. Only unit marking is the 416th patch adjacent to the nose numbers.

- A fuselage length increase of slightly over one foot (from 156 ft., 6.9 in. to 157 ft. 7.0 in.) for the installation of additional electronic countermeasures (ECM) equipment.
- The relocation of the tail-gunner from the rear of the aircraft to a rearward facing seat in the redesigned forward crew compartment.
- A redesign of the aft fuselage to eliminate the tail gunner's compartment and relocate the braking parachute compartment.
- A lightweight wing with integral fuel tanks replacing the bladder-type rubber cells in earlier models.
- Deletion of the manual aileron system (leaving only spoilers for lateral control).
- New 700-gal. fixed external fuel tanks replacing 3,000 gal. drop tanks near the wing-tip.
- A vertical stabilizer of 25% less span (91 in. lower).
- An improved water injection system with a larger 1,200 gal. water tank.
- An AN/ASG-15 defensive fire control system to replace the earlier MD-9 set.
- Enlarged ejection hatch windows at the pilot's stations.
- Aerodynamic ejection hatch lifters added to all stations except the pilots'.
- An increase of 19 tons in maximum gross take-off weight.
- Engine-driven hydraulic pumps and water injection pumps in place of the previous pneumatic packs.
- Ejection seats for the entire crew (the tail gunner previously did not have one).
- Electrically heated windows to prevent fogging and icing.
- Underwing pylons and systems, mounted between the inboard nacelles and the fuselage, permitting carriage of two nuclear-equipped North American GAM-77 Hound Dog air-to-surface missiles.
- A shorter one-piece nose radome instead of the previous two-piece unit, with an associated slight change in the nose contours.

With the B-52G, Boeing was determined to achieve a 15,000 lb. weight reduction compared to the B-52F. Using lighter alloys in the new wing design saved 5,847 lbs., and this coupled with eliminating the aileron system, shortening the vertical stabilizer, and eliminating the separate pressurized compartment for the tail-gunner ended up saving 15,421 lbs. The innovative wing structure involved machining long strips of aluminum so that stiffeners were an integral part of the structure. This resulted in a surface with a minimum of joints, greatly reducing the possibilities of leaks from the new integral fuel tanks. The new, smaller, non-jettisonable external wing tanks are considered an integral part of the aircraft and serve to stabilize the wing against flutter. A new trailing edge structure was also designed to minimize fatigue, and at the same time eliminate the manual ailerons previously located between the inboard and outboard flaps. Lighter weight flap drive motors were used, resulting in an increase in flap retraction time from forty to sixty seconds. The new shorter vertical stabilizer was flight tested on the first B-52A (52-001) during July 1957.

The new integral fuel tanks increased the fuel capacity of the wings by 8,719 gals., but due to the reduced size of the external tanks, the usable fuel capacity of the aircraft increased just 330 gals., to a total of 48,030 gals. The new fuel tanks required an entirely new fuel management system, including establishing a fuel sequencing operation so that flutter speed would always be well outside of the normal operating speed of the aircraft. The new fuel system was also decidedly simpler than the one it replaced.

As the basic fuselage of the new model 464-253 was essentially the same as that of its predecessors, there was no need for a mock-up of the entire aircraft. However, due to the major changes in the crew compartment, a full scale cabin mock-up was built. The new configuration, based on the "battle station" concept, placed the defensive crew (electronic warfare officer [EWO] and tail gunner) facing aft on the upper deck, and the offensive crew (navigator and radar-navigator) facing forward on the lower deck. The pilot and copilot stayed in their normal side-by-side positions on the flight deck. The floor structure in the pilot's footwells was lowered in order to accommodate folding rudder pedals, which improved pilot comfort and also partially eliminated over-controlling while taxiing since the pilot could now rest his heels on the cockpit floor. The pilots' seats and controls were moved forward slightly and the instrument panel was lowered and tilted for improved forward visibility.

In earlier models the heating system had deposited most of the heat on the flight deck, resulting in either the pilots roasting or the navigators freezing. A redesigned vent system attempted to cure this problem. The seats also were redesigned for more comfort on long flights, and additional "hot cups" for making soup or coffee were added. Numerous simplifications were made and automated features added to the electrical, hydraulic, and fuel systems, resulting in reduced crew workloads. The flight deck instrument panel arrangement was revised as a result of the simplifications, improving crew coordination, comfort, and mission capability. This configuration was inspected by the AF and approved during October 1956.

It should be noted that the changes were not altogether successful. The AF noted during Category II testing that temperature regulation in the crew compartment was still unsatisfactory, that the red lighting used was "...unduly harsh and causes eyestrain...", and that very limited storage space for extra flight equipment and personal items (thermos jugs, lunches, etc.) was available. Prob-

B-52G, 58-0177, lands at Wichita with drag 'chute deployed. Small markings on the vertical fin indicate locations of HF radio antenna.

B-52G, 58-0179, in typical 1970's finish. Cream color nose radome was typical. Yellow stripe on external tank is a leftover formation marking from 1972 "Bullet Shot" combat deployment to Guam.

B-52G, 58-0182, known as "Snowbird", was assigned to the Air Force Flight Test Center at Edwards AFB. Test programs flown by '0182 included SCAD and ALCM-A.

lems also were encountered with the design of the water bottles (they leaked), the main entry hatch (difficult to close), and the instructor pilot's seat (difficult to adjust). There also was some concern over the placement of caution and warning lights. Many of these problems are still true as of this writing (1989).

PRODUCTION

The AF received North American's and Boeing's proposals for WS-110A during October 1956. After five months of studying the proposals, both were found unacceptable and were rejected formally on March 11, 1957. The two companies re-submitted their respective WS-110A proposals during August 1957, and on December 23, 1957 North American Aviation was advised that they had won the competition. Their design was assigned the designation XB-70 two months later. Convair's proposed WS-125A nuclear powered bomber had been cancelled quietly several months earlier due to complex technical problems and a general lack of development funds. Therefore, it would fall on the B-70 to replace the B-52, or so it seemed.

By late 1957, when it had become all but certain that SAC's needs would not be fulfilled by the B-58, Congress and the AF agreed that it was both timely and necessary to move ahead with the long-anticipated B-52G as an interim measure pending the development of the B-70. In the meantime, with the scheduled completion of the last B-52F at Boeing's Seattle facility, production of future *Stratofortresses* would become the sole responsibility of Boeing's Wichita, Kansas plant which had been brought on-line as a second source for first-generation B-52s during early-1954. The rationale for switching all production to this facility was that it was unlikely there would ever again be sufficient orders to keep both plants operating at an economical capacity.

Once the decision was made to move ahead with the B-52G, three different procurement contracts were issued: AF33(600)-35992 for 53 aircraft funded during FY57; AF33(600)-34670 for 101 aircraft funded during FY58; and AF33(600)-37481 for 39 aircraft funded during FY59. The first contract was a cost-plus-incentive-fee (CPIF) type with a sliding 6% scale, and also covered non-recurring production engineering. It was initiated by letter contract on August 19, 1957 and finalized on May 15, 1958. The last two were fixed-price-incentive-fee (FPIF) contracts, the first started by a letter contract on June 14, 1957 and finalized on May 15, 1958, and the last begun by letter contract on September 5, 1958 and concluded on April 28, 1959.

Construction of the first aircraft (57-6468) got underway at Wichita during mid-1957 and progressed rapidly during the next year, entering final assembly on May 19, 1958. Following completion it was rolled out formally on July 23, 1958, and was the subject of extensive ground and taxi tests. It first flew on October 26, 1958 with Boeing-Wichita flight test manager Ray McPherson in the left seat.

Flight testing revealed that the performance of the B-52G was an improvement over the B-52F, even if it was not as great as hoped. However, troublesome stability problems (to be discussed later) were encountered throughout the flight envelope. Category II testing recommended a total of 9 "safety of flight" and 36 other items that needed fixing prior to the aircraft's introduction into operational service. Most of these deficiencies were minor, and easily corrected. Several never have been corrected completely.

As was the case with the B-52F, the B-52G failed to live up to original range estimates, suffering an approximate 8% deficiency at high altitude and 15% at lower altitudes. The range degradation was largely caused by the engine surge bleed valves opening at low altitude with a resultant loss of range (though they could also open above 45,500 ft. on the maximum range profile and during flight at maximum endurance power settings). The engine sound suppressors installed to reduce wing trailing edge structural failures also resulted in a range loss of approximately 3%. This was demonstrated by a maximum range mission where the test aircraft (57-6471) took off at 492,000 lbs., including a 16,160 lb. simulated bomb load, and flew a total of 7,959 n. miles without refueling. The original estimates for the same mission had indicated a range of 8,605 n. miles.

Concurrent with the on-going testing of the first B-52G, delivery of the first operational aircraft took place on February 13, 1959, when 57-6478 entered service[4] with the 5th Bomb Wing (BW) at Travis AFB. This event actually took place 12 days before the last B-52F from Seattle was delivered to the AF. During May, the 42nd BW became the second unit to receive the type, and by June 1959 no less than 41 B-52Gs had been delivered.

B-52G production ended during early 1961 with the AF accepting the last two aircraft during February. Fifty B-52Gs were accepted during FY59 (between October 1958 and June 1959); 106 during FY60 (between July 1959 and June 1960); and 37 during FY61 (between July 1960 and February 1961). As produced (i.e.; not counting in-service modifications) each B-52G cost $7.69 million, broken down as: $5,351,819 for the airframe; $1,427,611 for the engines; $66,374 for electronics; $6,809 for ordnance; and $840,000 for armament and miscellaneous items.

HOUND DOG AND QUAIL

Part of the original B-52G capability called for the carriage of two North American GAM-77 (AGM-28)[5] *Hound Dog* air-to-surface stand-off missiles.[6] A single missile could be transported under each wing. The missiles were attached to the aircraft with special pylons that were equipped with the necessary support, launch and control systems mounted internally. Though integral with the B-52G design, *Hound Dog* capability also was retrofitted to most first-generation B-52s. Although they incorporated structural provisions and wiring, the first 54 B-52Gs were delivered without *Hound Dog* capability, and later were modified to include it.

Hound Dog was a large weapon being approximately 43 ft. long with a 12 ft. wing span. Power was furnished by a single P&W J52-P-3 turbojet engine which enabled a top speed of 2.1 Mach and a maximum range at high

[4] This took place one day after the last Convair B-36 *Peacemaker* was retired from the AF inventory, creating an "all-jet" bomber force for SAC.

[5] The GAM-72 and GAM-72A were redesignated ADM-20A and ADM-20B, respectively, during 1962 as part of a DoD-wide designation rationalization, while the GAM-77 and GAM-77A became the AGM-28A and AGM-28B on the same date.

[6] The term "cruise missile" was not generally applied to air-launched weapons at this point, although the *Hound Dog* was simply a large cruise missile.

altitude of 700 miles. The missiles could be ignited while attached to the pylon, effectively giving the B-52 two additional engines. It was possible to refuel the missile from the B-52's internal fuel supply.

The McDonnell GAM-72 *Quail* was designed to carry an offensive system that enabled it to duplicate a B-52's radar signature and hence confuse and reduce the effectiveness of enemy radar-controlled air defense and infrared detection systems. The missile package as installed in the rear of the B-52 bomb bay consisted of a right and left launcher with two missiles per launcher. Naturally, performance closely duplicated that of the B-52 and speed varied from 0.6 Mach to 0.9 Mach while range was highly dependent on altitude (400 miles at 40,000 ft. to just 39 miles at extreme low levels). The missile could be reprogrammed to perform two heading changes and one variation in speed. Minimum launch altitude was 1,200 ft. above ground level. In addition to the B-52G/H, all B-52Es were retrofitted to carry the decoy.

To speed testing of the new B-52G missile systems several first-generation B-52s were modified as testbeds. A B-52D was used by McDonnell for early test launches of the *Quail*, while a modified B-52E (56-631) served as a testbed during much of the *Hound Dog's* integration and test phases. B-52Gs, of necessity, played an important role in the Category III (operational) testing of both the *Hound Dog* and *Quail*.

The first powered flight of a GAM-77 took place on April 23, 1959. The first full inertial-guided flight of a production *Hound Dog* occurred during October 1959 and the weapon officially entered service with SAC as WS-131B on December 21, 1959. Production of the improved GAM-77A began during 1961, and the original GAM-77 subsequently was removed from service.

Preliminary design of the *Quail* was started by McDonnell during 1955 and an extensive development flight test program was conducted at Holloman AFB and Eglin AFB with the first powered flight during November 1958. The GAM-72 test program concluded on June 24, 1960, and the missile was declared operational shortly thereafter. The first improved GAM-72A, with increased countermeasures capabilities and performance, was launched on November 18, 1960. Production GAM-72As began to enter service with SAC during September 1960, attaining operational status on February 1, 1961.

By the end of 1961, 400 GAM-72s and 225 GAM-77s had been delivered to SAC. Peak *Hound Dog* strength was attained during 1963 when SAC had just under 600 on hand out of a total 703 built. By the beginning of 1976 only 300 remained, and by the end of 1976 the missile had been withdrawn from service, replaced by the smaller but more reliable and accurate SRAM. *Quail* was removed from service during 1978.

B-52H

The B-52H (Boeing Model 264-261) does not differ outwardly from the B-52G, except for the shape of its engine nacelles and a slightly reconfigured aft fuselage to accommodate a new tail turret. An outgrowth of the B-52G, the B-52H design was initiated during January 1959, one month before SAC received its first B-52G. Although no great innovations resulted, some additional changes were made:

- Eight Pratt & Whitney TF33-P-3 turbofan engines.
- No water injection system was fitted (the TF33 does not use water injection).
- "Integrated flight instrumentation" for improved low-level flight capabilities.
- Advanced Capability Radar (ACR) with a terrain avoidance (TA) capability.
- New Sundstrand 120 KVA engine-driven generators.
- A new Emerson AN/ASG-21 fire control system.
- Small pylons installed between the two engine nacelles on each wing for AN/ALE-25 forward-firing chaff pods.
- A General Electric M61 *Vulcan* 20mm cannon with 1,180 rounds of ammunition replaced the earlier 0.50 caliber machine guns in the tail turret.
- Provisions for the never-to-be Douglas GAM-87A *Skybolt* air-launched ballistic missile.

The B-52H incorporated the turbofan version of the J57 engine, known in the commercial world as the JT3D, and designated TF33 by the military. The engine also was used on late versions of the Boeing 707 and Douglas DC-8 commercial transports and on the Lockheed C-141 military airlifter. The engine basically replaced the first three stages of the J57 compressor with a two-stage fan section. This enabled the engine to handle almost 2.5 times as much air, producing 50% more take-off thrust and 20% more cruise thrust. Specific fuel consumption decreased approximately 13%, going from 0.8 on the J57 to 0.56 on the TF33. A single B-52G, 57-6471, was fitted

Red Arkansas razorback hog and yellow "2" for Second Air Force identify 58-0189 as being from the 97th BW at the 1974 SAC Bomb Competition.

B-52G, 58-0189, of 320th BW at Mather AFB on Nov 6, 1987. Six AGM-84 "Harpoon" missiles are mounted on Heavy Stores Adapter Beam/stub pylon assembly.

B-52G, 58-0200, of 97th BW transient at Offutt AFB on Sept. 27, 1982. "Pop up" antenna for ALQ-117 stows mechanically when drag chute door opens.

B-52G, 58-0204, was believed to be testbed for the ALQ-172 or a competing ECM suite. It was also an AFFTC test airframe for AGM-86B and AGM-109 ALCMs.

with TF33 engines and utilized as a B-52H powerplant testbed during July of 1960. This aircraft quickly verified the new configuration's attributes.

With TF33s, the B-52H actually is overpowered in some flight regimes. Application of military rated thrust at light gross weights and traffic pattern speeds, coupled with the engines' placement forward of the center of lift, can result in a rapid, uncontrollable, pitch-up. As a result, B-52Hs are equipped with a mechanical thrust gate on the throttles. This adjustable gate is used as an aid in establishing reference power settings and to act as a throttle limiter for touch-and-go's, go-arounds, etc.

The B-52H airbrake lever added a detent at the "AIRBRAKES 1" position, which places the outboard spoiler groups up 10°. Thus more precise lateral control during air refueling could be attained—without pitch-up. The "AIRBRAKES 1" for air refueling procedure also is used by the B-52G even though it lacks the detent.

As originally installed in the B-52H (and retrofitted to B-52Gs and some B-52Ds at a cost of $313.2 million), the advanced capability radar (ACR) provided for terrain avoidance (TA), and included some anti-jamming and low-level mapping capabilities. The ACR gave three-dimensional information on three five-inch CRTs located in front of the pilot, copilot, and navigator. The ACR antenna was located in the extreme nose of the aircraft.

The addition of integrated flight instrumentation, which provided the pilot and copilot with independent primary flight reference systems, was a major improvement over the B-52G. The new "flight director system" was provided in part to assist the pilot during low-level penetration flights, and in part because the instrument panel had to be redesigned to incorporate the ACR's CRTs, which required a good deal of room in the center of the panel. An attitude director indicator (ADI) replaced the previous attitude indicator, glideslope indicator and turn and slip indicator. A horizontal situation indicator (HSI) also was provided, although it read heading references in five degree increments while the aircraft's navigation system provided this information in 0.5 degree increments. The ADI/HSI are identical to those used by the Northrop T-38 Talon. The B-52G subsequently was modified with identical instrumentation as well as the ACR with its terrain avoidance capabilities.

Two FPIF contracts, AF33(600)-38778 funded during FY60, and AF33(600)-41961 funded during FY61, accounted for the entire 102 aircraft B-52H production run. The first procurement, covering 62 aircraft, was initiated by letter contract on February 2, 1959 and finalized on May 6, 1960. The second contract was started by letter contract on July 28, 1960, but was not finalized until the latter part of 1962. The contract initially covered (and, as it ended up, totaled) 40 aircraft, but the AF did not want the contract finalized before it was sure that a sufficient number of aircraft were ordered since this was to be the last Stratofortress procurement.

The first B-52H (60-0001) made its initial flight on March 6, 1961, and the AF accepted it later the same month. By the end of June 1961, B-52H flight test had confirmed that the TF33 installation was performing more-or-less as predicted. Moreover, although the new Emerson AN/ASG-21 fire control system and the Sundstrand 120 KVA constant-speed generators needed perfecting, both were tactically operable. Testing also revealed, not surprisingly, that the B-52H suffered from the same directional stability problems as the B-52G. Many of the same complaints voiced about the B-52G were extended to the B-52H. These included unsatisfactory placement of caution and warning lights, cabin temperature control problems, and cockpit lighting. There also was considerable comment on the new flight instrumentation, mainly concerns over the marking of some instruments, and their general incompatibility with other aircraft systems (i.e.; the navigation system). A total of 20 items were thought to need ". . .immediate corrective action. . .", while 25 other items were deemed desirable to fix if practical.

The B-52H entered operational service with the 379th BW at Wurtsmith AFB, Michigan. The first aircraft (60-0001) was received by the 379th on May 9, 1961, and by the end of June there were 20 B-52Hs on hand. In contrast with most B-52Hs, the first 18 were not equipped during production for all-weather, low-level flying. However, modifications were accomplished between April and September 1962 that brought them up to the same standard as other production aircraft. Production ended during the fall of 1962, with SAC accepting the last B-52H (61-0040) on October 26, 1962. This aircraft went to the 4136th Strategic Wing (SW) at Minot AFB, North Dakota. In an attempt to maintain a reserve capability to reopen the production line if necessary, the AF negotiated a $770,283 agreement that ensured that Boeing would store the B-52H tooling until July 1963. Critical B-52 subcontractors, using government-owned facilities, would do the same. Nevertheless, 61-0040 would be the last B-52.

The AF accepted 20 B-52Hs during FY61 (from March through June 1961); 68 during FY62 (July 1961 to June 1962); and 14 during FY63 (the last five during October 1962). The flyaway cost per aircraft was put at $9.28 million, broken down as: $6,076,157 for the airframe; $1,640,373 for the TF33s; $61,020 for electronics; $6,804 for ordnance; and $1,501,422 for armament and miscellaneous items.

The Douglas GAM-87A Skybolt air-launched ballistic missile (ALBM) eventually was cancelled during December 1962, seemingly falling victim to political rather than technical considerations. Actually, Skybolt's demise was the result of many complex, interrelated elements, the chief two being rising costs and non-support by Secretary of Defense McNamara. The missile also suffered a number of test failures, which did not help matters. Each B-52H was to have carried four of the 1,000 mile range GAM-87As, two under each wing pylon.

Although the range of the B-52H was improved approximately 15% over the B-52G, it still fell short of estimates by some 7.5%. The new engines did give the aircraft markedly improved climb characteristics, however. As an example, the rate of climb for standard day sea level conditions at 350,000 lbs. and military power was 5,510 ft. per minute for the B-52H, compared to 4,000 ft. per minute for the B-52G. However, the climb performance improvement decreased with altitude and there was no significant difference between the B-52G and B-52H service ceilings.

By late-1961 several problems had become evident with the engine installation. Throttle creep, hang or slow starts, flameouts, and uneven throttle alignments were some of the most frequent problems. In addition, the engines consumed too much oil, turbine blades failed frequently and inlet cases often cracked. By mid-1962, even though most of these early problems had been corrected, the AF still wanted the engine to be more reliable and to achieve 600 hrs. between overhauls. Project Hot Fan, a $15 million depot level overhaul program, was initiated to accomplish these goals. Temporarily curtailed during the Cuban missile crisis, Hot Fan was resumed during January 1963, and all 894 TF33 engines in SAC's inventory had been modified by the end of 1964.

STRUCTURAL PROBLEMS

The B-52, like most other AF bombers, was designed to have a fatigue "life" of 5,000 flight hours. Maximum permissible load factors for the early aircraft were +2.0 g and no negative, although this was lowered somewhat as gross weight went up. The B-52 has greatly exceeded its original 5,000 hour life expectancy, and is currently targeted at something in excess of 15,000 hours. This extra time has not come easily and cheaply.

Somewhat coincident with the development of the B-52G, the rising threat of the immense Soviet surface-to-air missile (SAM) force initiated a reconsideration by the AF of the long-standing philosophy of high-altitude weapons delivery. In response, the Air Staff began a major reevaluation of delivery techniques, concluding that low-altitude approaches to heavily defended targets were considerably safer than high-altitude tactics. Directly affected by this change was the B-52 program, as it became necessary not only to optimize new aircraft for

B-52G, 58-0216, of the 42nd BW static at Offutt AFB in June 1981. Markings are standard SIOP scheme. SAC patch was normally on left, wing patch on right.

B-52G, 58-0219, at Castle AFB, November 1987. Blue/gray 93rd BW patch is on left side (standard for Strategic scheme). Gray "Castle" tail logo.

B-52G, 58-0222, of the 2nd BW at Barksdale AFB, April 29, 1987. Fleur-de-lis on fin is black. Barely visible "Barksdale" on external tank is dark gray.

B-52G, 58-0225, of the 2nd BW. Final approach view clearly shows extended position of Fowler flaps and landing gear doors.

the mission, but also to retroactively modify existing aircraft.

The nearly identical airframes shared by the B-52G and B-52H, designed in the strategic operating environment of the 1950s, were to have severe structural demands placed upon them by this new philosophy. These would precipitate the need for numerous structural modifications. The original designs, based on a high-altitude mission profile, proved inappropriate for the low-altitude requirement established during 1959, and the even lower-altitude terrain avoidance concept that surfaced during 1962. Little was known actually about the nature and effects of high-speed (but still subsonic), low-altitude, operations. Never before had a large aircraft, built for high-altitude operations, been recast into a completely foreign dynamic environment. In the case of the B-52G and B-52H, the AF and Boeing designated ten aircraft, five of each type, to "lead-the-fleet". This involved deliberately flying these aircraft on a higher percentage of missions than the rest of the fleet in order to accumulate time more rapidly. It was decided that the B-52G aircraft should have at least a 1,000 hour lead on the fleet, while the B-52Hs should lead by 1,500 hours.

By 1959, in response to the new low-altitude requirement, a *Stratofortress* modification program, referred to as "*Big Four*" (ECP-1000) was well underway. *Big Four* called for a major upgrade to each B-52's electronic warfare components, a strengthening of selected airframe components, and, on the B-52G, the incorporation of the B-52H's integrated flight instrumentation and advanced capability radar. This necessitated a rather involved reworking of the instrument panel in the B-52G to make it more-or-less identical with the B-52H's, but has ended up saving considerable effort over the years as additional systems (EVS, etc.) have been added.

During August 1962, just before the Cuban missile crisis, two of the B-52Hs at Homestead AFB, Florida, developed cracks where the wing was mated to the fuselage. Boeing soon determined that the ". . . primary contributing cause of these cracks was the use of taper lock fasteners throughout the forging. . .", which under high stress, and the high humidity around Florida, were susceptible to corrosion. Project *Straight Pin*, the modification package developed by Boeing, was raised to a high priority during September. During the rework, most of the fasteners around the wing-fuselage joint were replaced, and any small cracks around the holes removed by reaming. *Straight Pin* was completed by the end of 1962, despite being suspended for the missile crisis.

Intensive structural testing, conducted by Boeing and the AF during 1960 under ECP-0600, confirmed that hard usage, particularly low-level flying, shortened the structural life of the B-52. The extent of the fatigue problem was brought to light very dramatically on January 24, 1961 when a B-52G (58-0187), with only about 650 hours on the airframe, developed a massive fuel leak at high altitude. With JP-4 pouring out of the cracks in the lower wing skin, the pilot brought the aircraft in for a landing at Seymour Johnson AFB, South Carolina, but when full flaps were applied, the change in stress caused the wing to fold, resulting in loss of the aircraft.

The B-52G/H differed significantly from preceding models, but the design changes incorporated into the newer models made them even more susceptible to fatigue damage. The B-52G/H models were lighter than earlier B-52s, though their *gross* weights had been increased. Moreover, a portion of the overall decrease in structural weight had been achieved by using a lightweight aluminum alloy (T7178) in the aircraft's wings. While testing did not question the intrinsic strength of the wing, it pinpointed areas most likely to fatigue rapidly. No one could forecast accurately when the failures would happen, but low-level flying and the structural strains that occurred during air refueling were expected to speed up the fatigue considerably. The anticipated problems appeared serious enough for SAC to impose stringent flying restrictions on the new aircraft pending approval of necessary modifications.

During May 1961, the Air Staff endorsed a $219 million modification program for all B-52G and B-52H wing structures. The wing improvement program, carried out under ECP-1050, replaced the wing box beam with a modified wing box that used thicker aluminum of a different alloy (2024-T3511). It also installed stronger steel taper lock fasteners in lieu of the existing titanium fasteners, added brackets and clamps to the wing skins, added wing panel stiffeners, and made at least a dozen other changes. Finally, a new protective coating was applied to the interior surface of the integral wing fuel tanks. The program provided for Boeing to retrofit the modified wings during the aircraft's regular IRAN (Inspect and Repair as Necessary) schedule, except for the last 18 B-52Hs, which would receive the modifications on the Wichita production line. Started during February 1962, the program was completed more or less on schedule during September 1964, at a total cost of $139.1 million.

An older corrosion problem came to light again during August 1962. Two main landing gear outer cylinders failed on a B-52D and a B-52F, the latest in a series of similar incidents that also plagued the B-52G/H. While SAC immediately asked for a redesign of the cylinder,

B-52G, 58-0228, inflight with two AGM-28 "Hound Dog" missiles. Standard markings for 1960's period. "Hound Dogs" were painted gloss white.

B-52G, 58-0236, out of 379th BW (Wurtsmith AFB) visits Castle AFB on August 16, 1984. Standard markings and colors for period. Full color wing crest.

B-52G, 58-0239, of 416th BW rolls out at Griffiss AFB. Wrap around F.S. 36081 Gray is on nose. Replacement cowlings on #3 pod are also F.S. 36081 gray.

5th BW crew from Travis relaxing in front of B-52G, 58-0240, on September 7, 1960. White paint on fuselage roof was to aid in reducing heat in crew cabin.

B-52G, 58-0247, of AFFTC carries one AGM-109 Tomahawk ALCM on center aft station of left pylon. Strakelet wing root fairings were not yet added.

AF engineers noted that a quicker and safer alternative would be to use the existing design, but cast of a different alloy less susceptible to stress corrosion. This gave way during October to a new study and test program to further investigate current and potential stress corrosion problems. Meanwhile, to prevent other incidents, anti-corrosion paint was applied to all landing gear components.

By mid-1962, failure of the B-52H's constant speed drive was becoming a problem of the past. During this same period, a long-standing SAC requirement, initially endorsed only for the B-52H, finally was extended to all B-52s. Started during January 1963 and completed during March 1964, this retrofit program put two cartridge-type engine starters in every B-52. This installation was not as simple as it sounds. The aircraft's electrical system had to be modified to accommodate the new starters and valves, dust covers had to be redesigned, and nickel-cadmium batteries had to be added. The modification also was expensive, which accounted for SAC's difficulties in getting it approved for the entire B-52 fleet. Besides giving crews a means to start their engines quicker (by about 2 minutes), the new cartridge system allowed dispersed or post-strike B-52s to take off from airfields lacking ground support equipment. Although this was a giant step, SAC still was not satisfied with the amount of time it took the B-52H's TF33 engines to start. Project *Quick Start*, approved during 1974 added a cartridge starter to each of the B-52G and B-52H's eight engines, allowing a simultaneous starting of all engines and significantly improving reaction time. This project was completed during July 1976 and cost $35 million. *Quick Start* also introduced cartridge starters to all four engines on the SAC KC-135 fleet.

The AF also directed that the tail section of all B-52s should be reinforced in order to withstand turbulence during low-level penetration tactics. Started during September 1963, this engineering change (ECP-1124-2) was spread over a several year period. Another change, ECP-1128-1, strengthened the upper fuselage and further strengthened the vertical stabilizer at a cost of $87.9 million. Meanwhile, ECP-1185, costing about $65 million, was initiated during May 1966 and replaced the aircraft's fuselage side skin, crown skin fasteners, and upper longerons. Completion of this latest engineering change was accomplished during the aircraft's regular IRAN schedule.

During October 1967 the Air Staff approved ECP-1195, an engineering change that had been studied by SAC since 1965 and proposed by Boeing even earlier. Many of the improvements were in a direct answer to a problem unique to the B-52G/H uncovered during category II and III testing. When the vertical stabilizer had been shortened and the ailerons deleted in favor of an improved spoiler system, the aircraft failed to meet the military specifications for dynamic lateral-directional stability ("Dutch Roll"), as well as several other stability requirements. Although potentially dangerous, none of the conditions was considered a hazard to flight, and this partially accounted for the length of time required to initiate fixing the problem. Eventually known as the "B-52 Stability Augmentation and Flight Control" program, the $82.4 million modification installed a number of enhancements in the bombers to improve Dutch Roll damping, reduce structural loads, and improve controllability in turbulence. The modification provided higher performance rudder and elevator actuation systems and added stability augmentation system electronics. The change also deleted earlier magnetic yaw dampeners that were not considered effective. Necessary kits, contracted for during December 1967, began reaching the AF during mid-1969, and their installation required approximately two years.

Ensuring the durability of an airframe was a difficult and costly problem; a worse one, on both counts, was to cope with the enemy's technological developments.

During the early 1970s, many improvements in electronic countermeasures, initially limited to the Southeast Asia committed B-52Ds, were extended to the B-52G/Hs. These various projects centered on the installation of more efficient receivers and jammers to ease the penetration of enemy defenses. One project, *Rivet Rambler*, was a two-phase modification accomplished on all B-52Ds by 1971 and specifically directed against the SA-2 radars. The losses inflicted on the B-52Gs during *Linebacker II* convinced the AF to incorporate portions of *Rivet Rambler* in the B-52G/H. An interim measure involved fitting a Westinghouse AN/ALQ-119 ECM pod to the small pylons originally intended to carry the forward firing chaff pods. This modification, not nearly as easy as it sounds, was made to several Southeast Asia-committed B-52Gs. Fortunately, the Air Staff already had endorsed most of SAC's new requirements for the B-52G/H, with ECP-2525 to provide more efficient countermeasures equipment being approved during June 1971 and ECP-2519 (*Rivet Ace*) to upgrade the aircraft's radar warning receivers finally approved during December. Within a span of two years, the fairly unsophisticated *Rivet Ace* program would become a very ambitious endeavor, which still is continuing during 1989.

B-52G, 58-0258, flies a missed approach with the landing gear retracted. Full flaps in traffic pattern is typical, as are the soot deposits on flaps and wings.

B-52G, 59-2565, of 320th BW at Mather on November 6, 1987. "Ursa Minor" tail mark was a bear with sun rays—in black and F.S. 36118 gunship gray.

B-52G, 59-2570, "City of Bossier City" was 2nd BW entry in 1974 Bomb Comp. Winged "2" represented Second Air Force.

ALCM B-52G, 59-2571, at Castle AFB on August 28, 1984. Noteworthy is remarkably "clean" SIOP paint scheme—'2571 was one of the last so painted.

ALCM B-52G, 59-2584, of 97th BW, "Memphis Belle III". Black flaming torch on fin is representative of 97th BW insignia. Wing crest is dark blue and gray.

NEW CAPABILITIES

During November 1963, SAC issued requirements for a new short-range air-to-surface missile with a primary defense suppression mission and a secondary attack role. Boeing received authorization to proceed with technical development of the new missile on October 31, 1966 and the first live flights began during July 1969. On June 30, 1970 Boeing began procurement of production tooling and long-lead items, and on January 12, 1971 the AGM-69A Short Range Attack Missile (SRAM) was ordered into quantity production.

Required modifications and the addition of necessary equipment, such as wing pylons, launch gear, rotary launchers and new avionics, were accomplished by two different air materiel areas. Oklahoma City modified all B-52Gs, while San Antonio handled all B-52Hs. This $400 million modification program began on October 15, 1971 when a B-52G entered the Oklahoma City modification center. During March 1972 the first SRAM-equipped B-52G was delivered to the 42nd BW at Loring AFB.

Another project (ECP-1422) gave all B-52G/H aircraft the AN/ASQ-151 electro-optical viewing system (EVS) mounted in two turrets under the aircraft's nose. This system is composed of a Westinghouse AN/AVQ-22 low-light television unit mounted on the left and a Hughes AN/AAQ-6 forward looking infrared unit on the right. Designed to improve damage assessment and strike capabilities, the system also enhances terrain and hazard avoidance capabilities. This $248.5 million modification was installed by the San Antonio Air Materiel Area between 1971 and 1977. During 1983 a $29.0 million program was initiated to replace the FLIR's analog scan converter with a digital unit to improve reliabiltiy and reduce life-cycle cost.

The events leading up to the development of the EVS are noteworthy. During 1964, Boeing engineer Jack Funk installed a Sony TV camera on the tail of a flight test B-52 with a simple display on the flight deck. Funk demonstrated the system to Col. Rick Hudlow, and a SAC requirement was issued during late 1965 to study the feasibility of using visual sensors, including infrared, on the B-52 to improve damage assessment. A prototype development program with Boeing Wichita as the integration contractor was authorized during April 1969, and Hughes, Westinghouse, IBM, Kaiser, and Conrac were selected to provide elements of the system. Authorization to proceed with the limited engineering and long-lead procurement for qualification test articles was given during December 1970, and a production contract was finalized during June 1971. The last EVS modification kit was delivered by Boeing during early 1976, and installed at the San Antonio Air Logistics Center[7] shortly thereafter.

The AN/ASQ-38(V) bombing-navigation system carried by the B-52G/H had grown unreliable and difficult to repair by the mid-1970s. To remedy this situation the AF initiated a study of possible modifications during 1975, and actually started to upgrade the system during 1977. A prototype of the new AN/ASQ-176 offensive avionics system (OAS) first flew aboard a B-52G on September 3, 1980, and the first use of OAS to fire a live SRAM occurred on June 10, 1981. By January 1, 1984, contracts for 264 OAS kits had been let to cover 168 B-52Gs and 96 B-52Hs, and all aircraft had been updated by the end of 1986. The program had an estimated final cost of $1.662 billion.

The OAS is optimized for low-altitude operations, is substantially more reliable than the AN/ASQ-38(V), and is hardened to minimize the effects of nuclear electromagnetic pulse (EMP). The system is based around a Mil-Std-1553A digital data bus and includes new controls and displays, a new radar altimeter, an attitude heading reference system, an inertial navigation system, missile interface units, and substantial modifications to the attack radar.

An increase in fire power was obtained by the B-52G/H force when the AF selected the aircraft, along with the B-1, to carry the Air-Launched Cruise Missile (ALCM). Two contractors were in competition for the ALCM contract, Boeing with their AGM-86B, and General Dynamics with the AGM-109H Tomahawk derived from the Navy's submarine launched cruise missile. This $1.336 billion dollar program was started during early 1978 and a fly-off competition was staged during 1979 with Boeing being declared the winner. The first B-52G equipped with the AGM-86B was delivered to the 416th BW, which became operational with the weapon during December 1982.

The deployment to the 7th BW at Carswell AFB of the 131st B-52 (60-0055) capable of launching the ALCM on November 28, 1986 put the U.S. in violation of the unratified 1979 SALT-II treaty,[8] which limited the U.S. to 1,320 strategic nuclear delivery systems. The aircraft was the 33rd B-52H adapted to carry the AGM-86B, following 98 B-52Gs already deployed. A further 63 B-52Hs subsequently were modified by the San Antonio Air Logistics Center. ALCM-capable B-52Gs are fitted with a distinctive "strakelet" fairing at the leading edge of each wing root to give these aircraft a recognizable appearance in accordance with the provisions of the unratified SALT II agreement. ALCM-capable B-52Hs have a non-functional AN/ALT-32H "elephant ear" antenna on each side of the rear fuselage that projects straight out horizontally. These are located directly above the functional AN/ALQ-32H antennas which are angled downward from the lower curved fuselage side.

During 1979 the AF started modifying B-52G/Hs to carry AN/ASC-19 Air Force Satellite communications (AFSATCOM) equipment. This capability provides instantaneous world-wide command and control of forces and is designed to operate in both line-of-sight and satellite modes in the UHF frequency bands. The program cost $108.7 million.

Partially as a result of damage assessments of Argentine Exocet attacks on British ships during the Falklands war, the AF decided to equip four units of B-52Gs with the McDonnell Douglas AGM-84 Harpoon anti-ship missile. The four units were the 43rd BW based at Andersen AB on Guam, the 42nd BW at Loring AFB, the 320th BW at Mather AFB, and the 2nd BW at Barksdale AFB. The program was initiated during September 1982 when AF Chief of Staff Gen. Charles A. Gabriel and Chief of Naval Operations Adm. James D. Watkins signed a memorandum of agreement entitled "Joint USN/USAF Effort to Enhance USAF Contribution to Maritime Operations". By March 1983 the first B-52G had been modified to launch Harpoons, and three test launches were from high altitude (30,000 ft.) while the other was from 700 ft. and was directed by an E-3A AWACS. The first three modified aircraft were on station at Loring AFB by September 1983 and the modification program was completed during June 1985. The Harpoon modification made use of wiring originally installed for the SRAM, which was no longer used when external SRAM carriage was discontinued during the early-1980s.

A Collins Navstar Global Positioning System (GPS) was installed in a B-52G during late 1984 at Tinker AFB. Subsequently a 50 hr. flight test program was carried out at the Yuma Proving Grounds, Arizona, test range. The entire B-52G/H fleet is scheduled to receive similar equipment under a $45 million program initiated during 1986.

Beginning during 1985, all B-52Hs and some B-52Gs were equipped with the AN/APQ-166 "Strategic Radar" set, replacing the earlier OY-73/ASQ-176 radar set. This involved fitting new controls and displays, a new antenna electronics unit, an improved radar processor, and a modified radar antenna. Total cost of the modification was slightly in excess of $700 million.

On February 11, 1986, the USAF Aeronautical System Division began flight testing an integrated conventional stores management system (ICSMS) in a B-52G at McConnell AFB, Kansas. The ICSMS was developed by Boeing for installation in the 69 non-ALCM capable B-52Gs, permitting these aircraft to perform dual missions by carrying either nuclear or conventional weapons as required by rearranging data stored in the weapons systems computer by means of a preprogrammed removable software cassette. In addition, the aircraft's stub pylon/heavy stores beam was modified to permit the rapid integration of future weapons. The system is fully compatible with weapons developed under Mil-Std-1760. By the end of 1988, all 69 aircraft had been updated with the new sytem at a cost of $113 million.

The AF had planned to retire 98 B-52Gs during the early 1990s. However, during December 1987, Gen. John T. Chain, Commander in Chief, SAC, disclosed a possible plan for use of 160 B-52Gs to form a non-nuclear strike force. This was proposed as a means of filling the gap in NATO's defenses left by the elimination of medium-range nuclear weapons after the INF treaty was signed. The bombers would be combined with precision-guided munitions and could stand-off up to 200 miles

[7] The "Air Materiel Areas" were redesignated "Air Logistics Centers".

[8] In honor of this fact, the crew chief named the aircraft "SALT Shaker".

from their targets. The B-52G would carry twelve standoff weapons externally (similar to the *Harpoon* carriage), and 51 gravity bombs in their bomb bays. The bombers themselves would not be expected to penetrate deep into enemy territory. The upgrade was projected to cost $3 billion spread over seven years and limited AF approval for this project was given during June 1988. Possible weapons include the American developed Joint Tactical Missile System with a 50 mile range for use against hard targets, and an Israeli missile developed under the *Have Nap* program for use against tactical targets. The AF purchased 12 of the weapons during FY89 for further evaluation at a cost of $8.3 million. The 62nd BMS at Barksdale AFB gained a minimal capability with *Have Nap* during 1988-89.

The modifications to the B-52 have taken their toll on the aircraft's lift-to-drag ratio. The early B-52A/F had an L/D of approximately 21.0:1 while the initial B-52H had an approximately 19.0:1 L/D. The addition of 12 ALCMs and the EVS system lowered this further to 17.4:1, while with the EVS and 12 external SRAMs it dipped even lower to 17.0:1.

During September 1989 a total of 165 of the 193 B-52Gs built remained in the active inventory, 28 having been lost to various causes, including seven over Southeast Asia. Ninety-five of the 102 B-52Hs also remained in the inventory.

ODDS AND MODS

Boeing has studied and proposed reengining the B-52G/H several times over the years. The latest proposal calls for replacing the existing two-engine nacelles with single high-bypass turbofan engines in 757 sytle nacelles. The curent candidate engine is the Pratt & Whitney PW2037 (38,250 lbs. thrust) under the military designation F117-PW-100. Although the proposal seems to make good economic sense if the bombers are to be retained in service after the turn of the century, no definitive decision has been made.

SENIOR BOWL

Perhaps the least known of the external stores carried by the B-52H was the Lockheed D-21 drone. The sleek black drones originally were developed to be carried by two specially modified Lockheed A-12 (M-12) *"Black Birds"*. This aspect of the drone's operational career was short-lived due to difficulties with the launch procedures and political sensitivity (for the complete A-12/D-21 story, see *Aerofax Minigraph 1: Lockheed SR-71)*. Its fate was sealed when an M-12 and its launch control officer were lost during a D-21 test launch. The D-21 would make a return, this time being carried under the wings of two specially modified B-52Hs assigned to the 4200th Test Wing at Beale AFB, California. The two B-52Hs (thought to be 60-0021 and 60-0036) apparently were modified by the Oklahoma City Air Materiel Area during 1967-68. One photo has been released to date showing a B-52H carrying two D-21s, one under each wing on a pylon at the *Hound Dog* pylon attach point. All operational D-21 missions were launched from the B-52H aircraft under operation *"Senior Bowl"*. Although the project, run by the CIA, remains highly classified, it is thought flights were made over Southeast Asia and China during the late 1960s and early 1970s. The improving relations with China and the end of the Vietnam war, along with cost considerations, are thought to be the rationale for termination.

The D-21 was a low-signature ("stealth") drone 43 ft. 2 in. long with a 19 ft. wingspan. The drone weighed approximately 20,000 lbs. and had a top speed of 4.0 Mach. It was powered by a single Marquardt RJ43-MA-11 ramjet. After being dropped from the B-52H, a jettisonable solid-rocket booster installed under the drone would accelerate it to the speeds necessary for ramjet ignition, then fall away. It is thought that 38 vehicles were built by Lockheed between 1964 and 1969, and approximately 20 were attrited by the end of the program. The remaining drones initially were stored at Davis-Monthan AFB, Arizona, but were subsequently moved to an undisclosed location.

GIANT FISH

Two B-52H aircraft (60-0051 and 60-0052) based at Carswell AFB have provisions for an atmospheric sampling pod that can be loaded in the forward portion of the bomb bay. Two other B-52Hs (60-0024 and 60-0033) previously also had this capability, but subsequently have been demodified. A sampling control panel is mounted at the gunner's station near the gunner's right elbow. There is no degradation of defensive capability in *Giant Fish* aircraft.

The pod protrudes less than two feet below the bottom waterline of the aircraft. Five finger-like scoops face forward and provide the air intakes for a variety of particulate and radiation sampling systems inside the pod. On *Giant Fish* aircraft, the forward bomb door segments have a curved break line and the segments forward of this break line are removed when the pod is installed. For flight with the pod, the doors are deactivated and no internal weapons can be carried.

For *Giant Fish* missions, the B-52H crew is augmented by special equipment operators from the Air Force Technical Applications Center (AFTAC) at Patrick AFB, Florida. In the wake of the 1986 Chernobyl nuclear reactor accident in the Soviet Union, the two *Giant Fish* aircraft flew around-the-clock missions for several days, monitoring the spread of radiation in the atmosphere throughout the northern hemisphere. No incursions into Soviet airspace were made by the B-52Hs.

OPERATIONAL SERVICE:

RECORD FLIGHTS

On August 1, 1959, an AF crew landed their B-52G at Edwards AFB after completing a 28 hour, non-stop, flight of 12,942 miles. The flight had taken the bomber over all the capitals in the continental United States, plus Alaska and the District of Columbia. The aircraft recorded speeds in excess of 650 mph and altitudes in excess of 59,000 ft.

On December 14, 1960, a B-52G of the 5th BW, Travis AFB, completed a world record-breaking flight of 10,078.84 miles without refueling. The flight, dubbed project *"Long Jump"*, lasted 19 hours and 44 minutes and was commanded by Col. T. R. Grissom. The previous closed course record, established during 1947 by a B-29, had covered 8,854 miles.

On January 10-11, 1962, a B-52H of the 4136th SW at Minot AFB completed a record-breaking 12,532.28 mile unrefueled flight from Kadena AB, Okinawa, to Torrejon AB, Spain. Weighing 488,000 lbs. at take off, the B-52H flew at altitudes between 40,000 and 50,000 ft. with a top speed of 662 mph. The flight was commanded by Maj. Clyde P. Everly and was dubbed operation *"Persian Rug"*. This flight broke the old "distance in a straight line" world record of 11,235.60 miles held since 1949 by a Navy P2V named *"Truculent Turtle"*.

On June 7, 1962, a B-52H of the 19th BW at Homestead AFB, broke the world record for distance in a closed course without landing or refueling. The course had a validated distance of 11,336.92 miles, surpassing the old record of 10,078.84 miles held by a B-52G of the 5th BW.

COLD WAR

For many years during the 1960s, SAC kept a limited number of B-52s in the air around-the-clock in an effort to shorten reaction time in the event of war, ensure survivability of the force, and to demonstrate national resolve. The program started with considerable secrecy during early 1960, and 6,000 sorties had been flown by March 1962 when the program was made public. This airborne alert program was known as *"Chrome Dome"*, and each aircraft was fully armed with nuclear weapons. Each bomber would stay airborne for 24 hours, covering approximately 11,000 miles at an economical 400 knot cruising speed. During that 24 hour period, each aircraft was within striking distance of its target for 21 hours. The cost in fuel and spare parts for the program was estimated at $65 million per year, with fuel running $7,000 per aircraft per flight (kerosene was cheap then). There were plans at one point to expand the program to include 25% of the SAC bomber force, but the $750 million price tag curtailed the idea. Shortly after an accident at Thule, Greenland, the airborne alert program was terminated. This was only due in part to crashes experienced by the alert forces. Spiraling costs, rapidly accumulating airframe time, and the emergence of a large, highly-responsive, hardened, ICBM alert force with near 100% on-alert rates, led to the decision to terminate the program during 1968.

NUCLEAR ACCIDENTS

There have been two highly publicized B-52G accidents involving nuclear weapons. The first occurred on January 17, 1966 when a B-52G collided with a KC-135 tanker during a high-altitude refueling operation and both aircraft crashed near Palomares, Spain. Four of the 11 crewmembers survived. The aircraft carried four nuclear weapons, three of which were recovered soon after the accident. The fourth weapon, finally located by a U.S. Navy submarine about five miles from shore in approximately 2,500 ft. of water, ws recovered intact on April 7. The release of some radioactive material required the removal of some 1,400 tons of slightly contaminated soil and vegetation to the U.S. for disposal. Representatives of the Spanish government monitored the cleanup operations.

The second incident occurred on January 21, 1968 when a B-52G with four nuclear weapons aboard crashed and burned on the ice of North Star Bay while attempting an emergency landing at nearby Thule Air Base, Greenland. Six of the seven crew members survived. All four nuclear weapons were destroyed by fire. Some radioactive contamination occurred in the area of the crash, and approximately 237,000 cubic ft. of contaminated ice, snow, and water, along with the crash debris, was removed and transported to approved U.S. storage sites. The cleanup operation was completed on September 13, and no traces of excessive radioactivity subsequently were found. Representatives of the Danish government monitored the cleanup operations.

SOUTHEAST ASIA

B-52Fs first arrived for operation *"Arc Light"* during 1965 and B-52 conventional bombing operations over Southeast Asia (SEA) increased every year thereafter. B-52Gs did not enter the war before mid-1972, yet their short-lived participation did not prove easy. The deployment of B-52Gs to Andersen AB on Guam were known as *"Bullet Shot"* missions. On December 18, 1972 President Nixon ordered B-52Gs and the older B-52Ds to begin bombing military targets in the Hanoi and Haiphong areas of North Vietnam as part of *"Linebacker II"*. In the attacks on Haiphong and Hanoi, the B-52s encountered awesome air defenses, and in 11 days, 15 B-52s were shot down by surface-to-air missiles, mainly SA-2 *Guidelines*. SAC lost seven B-52Gs in SEA, all of them during *Linebacker II*. Six of the aircraft were downed by enemy SAMs over North Vietnam, four of them going down around Hanoi and the other two crashing in Thailand. The seventh B-52G loss was only indirectly caused by the war when the aircraft crashed into the ocean after taking off from Andersen AB.

On December 26, all Andersen AB aircraft, 33 B-52Ds and 45 B-52Gs, were launched in a compressed two hour and twenty-nine minute period. Four waves of these aircraft, from four directions, would converge at the same instant over Hanoi while three additional waves would strike Haiphong. There were 120 targets, all with the same bomb release time. The mission was supported by 113 other aircraft, ranging from Douglas EB-66s and Grumman EA-6As to Republic F-105G *Wild Weasels*. Despite heavy SAM defensive firing, the attack went off as planned, and "only" two B-52s were lost. For the next two days the B-52s returned to destroy individual SAM sites located on the 26th. On December 29 orders came terminating *Linebacker II*. The North Vietnamese had returned to the negotiating table, and the end of the United State's involvement in the war was in sight.

Going into *Linebacker II*, the AF calculated their "acceptable" losses at 3%. As it turned out, the losses amounted to "only" 2%—15 aircraft out of 729 sorties flown. In fact, four of the B-52Gs lost were downed on the same mission. The damage total for the raids was 383 rail cars, 14 locomotives, 191 warehouses and two major bridges destroyed. Additionally, 75 or so other buildings were destroyed or badly damaged.

SAC B-52s terminated eight years of conventional bombing operations over Southeast Asia on August 15, 1973, when all U.S. bombing of targets in Cambodia ceased. The various B-52s (D, F, and G) had logged 126,615 sorties in SEA, expending an incredible 2.63 million tons of ordnance at a cost of 17 aircraft to enemy defenses and 12 more to other operational causes. Of the total sorties, 55% hit targets in South Vietnam, 27% in Laos, 12% in Cambodia and just under 6% in North Vietnam (almost all during *Linebacker II*).

SIGNIFICANT INCIDENTS

Boeing flew a heavily instrumented B-52H (61-0023) in a series of test flights that resulted in one of the most published photos ever taken of a B-52. The Boeing crew, commanded by instructor pilot Charles F. "Chuck" Fisher, was engaged in an eight hour flight over mountainous terrain at a 500 ft. altitude. During the tests, the turbulence became so extreme that the crew decided to discontinue the mission and climb to 14,000 ft. At that altitude, a sudden five second blast of clear air turbulence moved the aircraft sharply to the right and collapsed the

ALCM B-52G, 59-2584, landing at Griffiss AFB, New York. Drag chute deployment is normal full stop landing procedure. Ground runs with drag chute were typically about 5,000 feet on a dry runway.

B-52G, 59-2588, of the 2nd BW at Barksdale. Stub pylon is mounted and configured with two Multiple Ejector Racks (MERs). Standard Strategic paint with subdued 2nd BW patch on nose.

vertical fin.

At Wichita a group of experts gathered, and a KC-135 tanker was dispatched for possible inflight refueling while test pilot Dale Felix scrambled in a North American F-100 chase aircraft. When Felix joined up with the crippled bomber what he saw was that the turbulence had completely sheared off the bomber's rudder and 85% of its vertical stabilizer! A quick check of air bases revealed that Blytheville AFB offered an approach over unpopulated areas and had the wind blowing straight down the runway. Fisher brought the aircraft in, flaps up, without incident. Data from the recorders provided invaluable assistance in determining structural improvements to help the B-52 withstand similar incidents in the future. Aircraft 61-0023 still is in service, with the 5th BW at Minot AFB, and is the lowest time B-52H in the SAC inventory.

On December 28, 1984, a B-52G (57-6484) received substantial fuselage damage when the forward gear retracted inadvertently during the takeoff roll, skidding to a stop beyond the paved runway overrun at Loring AFB. There was extensive damage to the fuselage extending from the EVS turrets to the bomb bay. The fuselage almost separated into two sections, breaking in the water tank area immediately aft of the crew compartment. The flightcrew evacuated the airplane through an upper escape hatch. Since there were a limited number of B-52Gs in the fleet, it was decided to repair the aircraft instead of writing it off. The aircraft removal from the overrun was initiated by separating the crew compartment from the rest of the fuselage. Wiring, tubing, and cables were disconnected whenever possible instead of cutting them. The fuselage then was lifted with a crane and the forward gear manually extended. To reduce costs, major fuselage sections were salvaged from a retired B-52F at Davis-Monthan AFB. Other assemblies were taken from the airframe mockup and the AF logistics system and several thousand parts had to be fabricated from scratch. During early July 1985, fifty-five Boeing engineers and technicians started the task of rebuilding the aircraft. After 11 months of work, the aircraft took to the air on May 27, 1986.

WING HISTORIES

2nd Bombardment Wing (Barksdale AFB, Louisiana)—Activated during 1963 at Barksdale AFB with a squadron of B-52Fs, the 2nd BW converted to the B-52G on June 25, 1965 with the addition of the 62nd BMS from Eglin AFB. On the same date, the 20th BMS and its B-52Fs were transferred to the 7th BW at Carswell AFB. The 2nd became a "super" wing effective April 25, 1968 when it gained the 596th BMS and its B-52Gs from Dow AFB, Maine. Both the 62nd and 596th squadrons remain active in the wing as of late 1989. The 62nd is a conventional-only unit with *Harpoon* capability, while the 596th's B-52Gs are both conventional and external ALCM capable. The wing also includes the 2nd, 32nd, and 71st Air Refueling Squadrons (AREFS).

5th Bombardment Wing (Travis AFB, California/Minot AFB, North Dakota)—At Travis AFB, the 5th BW was the first SAC wing to receive production B-52Gs, with the first aircraft (57-6478) arriving on February 13, 1959. Initially both the 23rd and 31st BMSs were assigned, with a total of 30 B-52Gs, but on October 1, 1959 the 31st was reassigned to the 4126th SW and moved to Beale AFB in the following weeks. During the summer of 1968 the 5th phased down its B-52G operations, transferring the aircraft to the 320th BW at nearby Mather AFB. On July 25, 1968, the wing's designation was moved, without personnel or equipment, to Minot AFB, where it replaced the B-52H equipped 450th BW. At Minot the 5th began taking delivery of SRAM missiles on September 28, 1973, and was declared operational with SRAM on December 31. During 1980, the 5th became part of the Strategic Projection Force (SPF), SAC's contribution to the Rapid Deployment Force (RDF) and Rapid Deployment Joint Task Force (RDJTF). Shortly thereafter, the wing's fleet of B-52Hs were modified for internal and external conventional stores carriage and received OAS. During 1988 the wing added ALCM and during 1989, Strategic Radar. The wing currently consists of the 23rd BMS and 906th AREFS.

7th Bombardment Wing (Carswell AFB, Texas)—The 7th BW began flying new production B-52Fs during 1958 with the 9th BMS and, briefly, the 492nd BMS. The 20th BMS joined the wing during 1965 with another squadron of B-52Fs. During 1968 the 9th was inactivated and the 20th converted to the B-52D. During 1972 the 9th rejoined the wing with the B-52D. On May 3, 1982, the first B-52H (61-0018) arrived at Carswell marking the start of the 9th's conversion from B-52Ds. On October 1, 1982 the 9th assumed alert with four B-52Hs. During the summer of 1983, crews from the 20th transitioned to the B-52H and the wing ceased B-52D operations on October 1, 1983. During 1984 the wing's B-52Hs began receiving OAS, followed by ALCM and Strategic Radar during 1986. As of 1989 the wing's flying squadrons remain the 9th and 20th BMSs and the 7th AREFS. During November of 1989 it was announced that the 7th BW would become one of two B-52G/H Wings to be equipped with the new stealth—optimized Advanced Cruise Missile.

17th Bombardment Wing (Wright-Patterson AFB, Ohio/Beale AFB, California)—The 17th BW and 34th BMS converted from the B-52E to the B-52H during June/July 1968, with the B-52Hs coming from the inactivating 19th BW at Homestead AFB. During the summer of 1975 the wing began phasing down for inactivation at Wright-Patterson. On September 30, 1975, the wing moved in name only to Beale, replacing the 456th BW. At Beale the 17th flew B-52Gs for one year and was finally inactivated on September 30, 1976. Subsequently the wing was redesignated as the 17th Reconnaissance Wing and on October 1, 1982 activated at RAF Alconbury with TR-1s.

19th Bombardment Wing (Homestead AFB, Florida/Robins AFB, Georgia)—After phasing out B-47 operations during 1961, the 19th BW prepared for conversion to B-52s, with the first B-52H (61-0005) arriving at Homestead AFB on February 7, 1962. Beginning during early June 1968, the wing began transferring its B-52Hs to the 17th BW at Wright-Patterson AFB. On July 25, 1968, the wing and 28th BMS were transferred, without personnel or equipment, to Robins AFB, replacing the 465th BW and 781st BMS. The 19th flew the B-52G at Robins until October 1, 1983 when the 28th was inactivated and the wing redesignated the 19th Air Refueling Wing.

28th Bombardment Wing (Ellsworth AFB, South Dakota)—After operating B-52Ds since 1956, the 28th BW converted to the B-52G during early 1971, concurrent with the drawdown of the 72nd BW at Ramey AFB. After combat deployments to SEA, the 28th transitioned from being a single squadron B-52G wing to a two-squadron B-52H wing. The 28th's B-52Gs were transferred to the 379th BW at Wurtsmith AFB in exchange for that unit's B-52Hs. The addition of B-52Hs from the inactivating 449th BW enabled the wing to activate the 37th BMS on July 1, 1977 to join the established 77th BMS. On October 1, 1982 a major SAC reorganization saw the 37th inactivated. At the same time, the 28th picked up the Strategic Projection Force commitment previously held by the 319th BW which simultaneously converted to the ALCM B-52G. During October 1985 the 28th began phasing out B-52H operations in preparation for the wing's 1987 conversion to the B-1B.

39th Bombardment Wing (Eglin AFB, Florida)—Activated February 1, 1963, the 39th BW replaced the 4135th SW, primarily committed to test support activities at Eglin. On June 25, 1965 the wing was inactivated, but its 62nd BMS moved with its B-52Gs to Barksdale AFB and joined the 2nd BW.

42nd Bombardment Wing (Loring AFB, Maine)—After initially equipping as a three-squadron B-52C/D wing during 1956, the 42nd BW took delivery of 30 B-52Gs with the first (57-6500) arriving on May 21, 1959. The B-52Gs were delivered to the 69th and 70th BMSs in two groups: the first during the summer of 1959 and the second trickling in between November 1959 and January 1961. On June 25, 1966, the 70th and 15 of the B-52Gs were shifted to Plattsburgh AFB as the 528th BMS. From 1972 the 42nd BW was the first SAC wing to receive the SRAM, EVS, and the Phase VI ECM package. The wing was declared operational with SRAM on September 15, 1972. During the mid-1980s, the wing added OAS and *Harpoon* missiles to its arsenal. During 1988 the wing was released from its SIOP commitment, becoming one of four purely conventional-tasked units. During 1989 the wing's squadrons were the 69th BMS and the 42nd and 407th AREFSs.

43rd Strategic Wing/43rd Bombardment Wing (Andersen AB, Guam)—Activated on April 1, 1970 at Andersen AB, the 43rd SW initially was equipped with B-52Gs and played host to the strategic air armada assembled via *"Bullet Shot"* deployments during 1972 for the *Linebacker* campaigns. Converted to the B-52G during the summer of 1983, removing SAC's last B-52D from alert on October 1, 1983. On November 4, 1986, the wing was redesignated the 43rd Bombardment Wing, Heavy. Released from nuclear commitments and alert during April 1988. The 60th BMS currently is active with the B-52G/*Harpoon*. The unit is scheduled to be inactivated on June 15, 1990.

68th Bombardment Wing (Seymour Johnson AFB, North Carolina)—Activated with B-52Gs on April 15, 1963 along with the 51st BMS, replacing the 4241st SW. The wing and its entire force of B-52G/KC-135A aircraft deployed to SEA on June 27, 1972 for *Linebacker* operations, returning to Seymour Johnson during July 1973. During the summer of 1982 the wing phased out B-52G operations, and on September 30, 1982 the wing and 51st BMS were inactivated. The 68th was reactivated on the same date as the 68th Air Refueling Group. Redesignated the 68th Air Refueling Wing on October 1, 1986, the wing is currently operational with two squadrons of McDonnell Douglas KC-10 tankers.

72nd Bombardment Wing (Ramey AFB, Puerto Rico)—The 72nd BW phased out its last B-36 during 1958 in preparation for conversion to the B-52G, and the first aircraft (58-0168) arrived on August 14, 1959. During the spring of 1971 the wing transferred its aircraft out (mostly to the 28th BW at Ellsworth AFB) and was inactivated on June 30, 1971.

B-52G, 59-2596, of 43rd Strategic Wing at Andersen AFB, Guam, on May 12, 1985. Heavy Stores Adapter Beam (HSAB) is mated to stub pylon under wing. White noses were becoming rare by this time.

92nd Strategic Aerospace Wing/92nd Bombardment Wing (Fairchild AFB, Washington)—Equipped with B-52Ds from 1956 (325th, 326th, and 327th BMSs), the wing and its one remaining squadron (325th) converted to the B-52G during late-1970/early-1971, concurrent with the phase down of B-52G operations at Plattsburgh AFB. On March 21, 1972 the wing was redesignated as the 92nd Bombardment Wing, Heavy. During June 1972 the wing deployed its bomber force to SEA for *Linebacker* operations, returning to Fairchild on October 24, 1973. During 1983 the wing added ALCM to its B-52Gs. On September 10, 1985 the first B-52H (60-0032) arrived from the San Antonio ALC marking the start of the wing's conversion from ALCM B-52Gs to ALCM B-52Hs. The 92nd currently is operational with the 325th BMS and the 43rd and 92nd AREFSs.

93rd Bombardment Wing (Castle AFB, California)—The 93rd BW introduced the B-52 to SAC on June 29, 1955 and has flown every SAC model from the B-52B to the B-52H. Since that date the wing has been SAC's "schoolhouse" for combat crew initial qualification training. During 1974 the 93rd phased out its last B-52F and equipped with a mix of B-52G and B-52H models. Crew training was model specific until 1983 when the B-52Hs were returned to operational units and all Castle bomber training was standardized on the B-52G. For the entire period with the B-52G/H, the 328th BMS has been the "flight line" squadron, while the 4017th Combat Crew Training Squadron (redesignated 329th CCTS during 1985) provides academic training. Other organizations include the 330th Central Flight Instructor Squadron (Central Flight Instructor Course—CFIC), the SAC Instrument Flight Course (SIFC) and the 93rd and 924th AREFSs.

96th Bombardment Wing (Dyess AFB, Texas)—During the summer of 1982, the 96th BW and its 337th BMS converted from the B-52D to the B-52H, changing over alert to the B-52H on October 1, 1982. The wing had a very short history in the B-52H, phasing down in the fall of 1984 with the last B-52H moving to Carswell AFB on January 22, 1985 in preparation for conversion to the B-1B.

97th Bombardment Wing (Blytheville [renamed Eaker] AFB, Arkansas)—Activated on July 1, 1959 at Blytheville AFB, having moved from Biggs AFB, Texas, after disposing of B-47s. The wing's first B-52G (58-0221) was delivered on January 9, 1960. Deployed to Guam from mid-1972 until October 1973. Added ALCM in 1984. The wing's 340th BMS remains current with the B-52G/ALCM and is joined by the 97th AREFS.

319th Bombardment Wing (Grand Forks AFB, North Dakota)—The 319th BW took over the personnel and equipment of the 4133rd SW on February 1, 1962. Activated simultaneously was the 46th BMS. The wing added SRAM capability to its B-52H force in 1973, and in 1980 formed (with the 5th BW) the Strategic Projection Force. In conjunction with the SPF assignment, the 319th was the first to receive the OAS and full conventional weapon modifications. In 1982 the B-52Hs were replaced by ALCM-capable B-52Gs which the wing flew until December 4, 1986 when the last aircraft departed and the wing began preparations for converting to the B-1B.

320th Bombardment Wing (Mather AFB, California)—The 320th BW was activated on February 1, 1963 at Mather AFB, replacing the 4134th SW. In the summer of 1968, the 320th and its 441st BMS converted from the B-52F to the B-52G. In June 1972 the wing deployed to Guam for Linebacker combat operations, returning home in October 1973. In 1988 the 320th became one of SAC's four dedicated conventional wings. In July 1989 the wing ceased operations with the B-52G, and inactivated on September 30, 1989.

379th Bombardment Wing (Wurtsmith AFB, Michigan)—Activated on February 9, 1961 at Wurtsmith AFB, moving from Homestead AFB, Florida, where it had been a B-47 wing. On May 9, 1961 SAC's first B-52H (60-0001 - "The State of Michigan") arrived. In 1977 the wing converted to the B-52G in a swap of aircraft with the 28th BW and in 1982 became SAC's second ALCM wing. The 379th, with its 524th BMS and 920th AREFS, remains active at Wurtsmith.

380th Strategic Aerospace Wing (Plattsburgh AFB, New York)—With the arrival of the assets from Loring AFB's 70th BMS (to form the 528th BMS), the 380th SAW competed its transition from the B-47 to the B-52G in the summer of 1966. The wing's B-52 history was short, with the last B-52G departing Plattsburgh on 5 January 1971 in preparation for converting to the FB-111A.

397th Bombardment Wing (Dow AFB, Maine)—The 397th BW replaced the 4038th SW at Dow AFB on February 1, 1963. The wing's B-52Gs were operated by the 596th BMS, activated on the same day. On April 25, 1968, the wing's entire B-52G and KC-135 force and flying squadrons were transferred to the 2d BW at Barksdale AFB, the 397th was inactivated, and Dow AFB was closed.

410th Bombardment Wing (K. I. Sawyer AFB, Michigan)—The 410th BW and the 644th BMS were activated on February 1, 1963 and replaced the 4042d SW/526th BMS. The 410th has flown the B-52H continuously since that date. The wing was the first B-52H unit to receive SRAM and the Phase VI ECM modifications. From 1987 the wing added the AN/ALQ-172 ECM package and modifications to support the AGM-129A advanced cruise missile. Current at K. I. Sawyer AFB with the 644th BMS and the 46th and 307th AREFSs.

416th Bombardment Wing (Griffiss AFB, New York)—Activated on February 1, 1963 at Griffiss AFB, the 416th BW replaced the 4039th SW and gained that wing's B-52Gs. The wing and its 668th BMS have flown the B-52G since. On January 11, 1981 the wing received its first AGM-86B ALCM, followed by the first ALCM-capable B-52G (58-0247) on August 15, 1981. Together with cruise missile integration, the 416th's were the first B-52Gs to receive OAS. After an extensive ALCM activation program, the wing began standing alert with ALCMs on December 16, 1982. Still at Griffiss, the wing consists of the 668th BMS and the 41st AREFS.

449th Bombardment Wing (Kinross [renamed Kincheloe] AFB, Michigan)—The 449th BW was activated on February 1, 1963, replacing the 4239th SW at Kincheloe AFB. The wing's 716th BMS operated B-52Hs until July 20, 1977 when the last one was transferred to Ellsworth AFB. The 449th BW and the 716th BMS were inactivated on September 30, 1977, as Kincheloe AFB went into caretaker status and closure.

450th Bombardment Wing (Minot AFB, North Dakota)—The 450th BW replaced the 4133rd SW at Minot on February 1, 1963. Activated simultaneously with the wing was the 720th BMS. The 450th and 720th were in turn replaced on July 25, 1968 by the 5th BW/23rd BMS.

456th Strategic Aerospace Wing/456th Bombardment Wing (Beale AFB, California)—The 456th SAW took over from the 4126th SW at Beale AFB on February 1, 1963. The 744th BMS also activated to operate B-52Gs. On July 1, 1972 the wing was redesignated 456th Bombardment Wing, Heavy. On September 30, 1975, the 456th BW and 744th BMS were inactivated and replaced by the 17th BW and 34th BMS.

465th Bombardment Wing (Robins AFB, Georgia)—Activated on February 1, 1963, replacing the 4137th SW. The 781st BMS was assigned to operate the wing's B-52Gs. On July 25, 1968 the wing and squadron were inactivated and replaced by the 19th BW and 28th BMS.

4038th Strategic Wing (Dow AFB, Maine)—Activated at Dow AFB on August 1, 1958. On February 15, 1960 the 341st BMS was activated and on May 27, 1960 the first B-52G (58-0252) was delivered to the unit. On February 1, 1963, the 4038th SW and 341st BMS were inactivated and replaced by the 379th BW and 596th BMS.

4039th Strategic Wing (Griffiss AFB, New York)—Activated at Griffiss AFB on August 1, 1958. The 75th BMS was added on 15 October 1959 in preparation for B-52G deliveries, which began with 58-0225 on January 12, 1960. On February 1, 1963, the wing and squadron were inactivated and replaced by the 416th BW and the 668th BMS.

4042d Strategic Wing (K. I. Sawyer AFB, Michigan)—The 4042d SW was activated on August 1, 1958, but had no tactical squadrons for almost two years as facilities were built. After the activation of an air refueling squadron in 1959, the 526th BMS was activated on June 1, 1961 and final preparations for the arrival of B-52Hs were completed. The wing's first B-52H (60-0024) was delivered on July 31, 1961. On February 1, 1963 the wing and squadron were inactivated and replaced by the 410th BW and 644th BMS.

4126th Strategic Wing (Beale AFB, California)—On February 8, 1959 the 4126th SW was activated at Beale AFB in preparation for assignment of B-52 and KC-135 aircraft. On October 1, 1959 the 31st BMS was assigned to the wing, though still operating at Travis AFB. On October 26, 1959 the 31st formally was assigned to Beale, while the aircraft and crews gradually arrived between November 1959 and January 1960. The 4126th SW and 31st BMS were inactivated on February 1, 1963 and replaced by the 456th

B-52G, 59-2598, of 42nd BW, September 8, 1988 at Plattsburgh AFB, NY, airshow. Black moose with blue bomb was Loring bomber tail marking for period. "Loring" on tanks also in blue.

Unidentified B-52G during gear retraction sequence on takeoff with test radomes below cockpit and on upper fuselage. Also noteworthy are small raked fins mounted on horizontal stabilizers.

Remains of B-52G 59-2597 after explosion and fire consumed it on Castle AFB runway. Hot fluid from ruptured hydraulic line started fire in forward wheel well which led to explosion.

George Cockle Collection

ALCM B-52G being towed into position on trestle, the electromagnetic pulse test facility at Kirtland AFB, New Mexico. Trestle tests EMP "hardness" of aircraft and systems.

SAW and 744th BMS.

4133rd Strategic Wing (Grand Forks AFB, North Dakota)—Activated at Grand Forks AFB on September 1, 1958. Initially equipping with KC-135s (905th AREFS), the 30th BMS was activated on January 1, 1963 and the first B-52H (61-0015) arrived on April 20, 1962. Inactivated on February 1, 1963 and replaced by the 319th BW and 46th BMS.

4135th Strategic Wing (Eglin AFB, Florida)—Activated on December 1, 1958 at Eglin AFB. Gained the 301st BMS on June 17, 1959 and received their first B-52G (58-0161) on July 24, 1959. Primarily charged with development and test operations. Inactivated on February 1, 1963 and replaced by the 39th BW and 62d BMS.

4136th Strategic Wing (Minot AFB, North Dakota)—Activated on September 1, 1958. Gained the 525th BMS on March 8, 1961 and received its first B-52H (60-0025) on July 13, 1961. Inactivated on February 1, 1963, replaced by the 450th BW. The 525th concurrently was replaced by the 720th BMS.

4137th Strategic Wing (Robins AFB, Georgia)—Activated on February 1, 1959. Gained the 342d Bomb Squadron on May 1, 1960. The wing's first B-52G (59-2575) arrived from Boeing Wichita on August 4, 1960. Inactivated on February 1, 1963 and replaced by the 465th BW and 781st BMS.

4239th Strategic Wing (Kinross [renamed Kincheloe] AFB, Michigan)—Activated at Kinross AFB on February 1, 1959. On August 1, 1961 the 93rd BMS was activated. The first B-52H assigned to the wing was 60-0044. Inactivated on February 1, 1963 and replaced by the 449th BW and 716th BMS.

4241st Strategic Wing (Seymour Johnson AFB, North Carolina)—Activated on October 1, 1958. Added the 73rd BMS on January 5, 1959. Received their first B-52G (58-0158) on July 24, 1959. Inactivated on 15 April 1963 and replaced by the 68th BW and 51st BMS.

SQUADRON HISTORIES

9th Bombardment Squadron (7th BW - Carswell AFB)—The 9th BMS converted from the B-52D to the B-52H during the summer of 1982, with the unit's first B-52H arriving on May 3, 1982. After assuming alert in the B-52H on October 1, 1982, the 9th subsequently added OAS (from 1984), ALCM and Strategic Radar (from 1986). Current with B-52H.

20th Bombardment Squadron (7th BW - Carswell AFB)—The 20th BMS converted from the B-52D to the B-52H during the summer of 1983, with an operational history paralleling that of the 9th BMS. Current with B-52H.

23rd Bombardment Squadron (5th BW - Travis AFB [G], Minot AFB [H])—The 23rd BMS, as part of the 5th BW at Travis AFB, was the first unit to equip with the B-52G, converting from the B-36. The squadron's first B-52G (57-6478) arrived on February 13, 1959. During the summer of 1968, the squadron's B-52Gs were transferred gradually to the 320th BW at Mather AFB. On July 25, 1968 the 23rd moved, without personnel or aircraft, to Minot AFB, replacing the 720th Bomb Squadron with B-52Hs. Took delivery of their first SRAM missiles on September 28, 1973 and added SRAM to their alert force on 31 December 1973. At Minot the 23rd was one of the original units comprising the Strategic Projection Force (SPF). Added ALCM from 1988 and Strategic Radar from 1989. Current with B-52H.

28th Bombardment Squadron (19th BW - Homestead AFB [H], Robins AFB [G])—At Homestead AFB, the 28th BMS was one of the original six B-52H units, receiving their first aircraft (61-0005) on February 7, 1962. During June and July 1968 the 28th transferred its B-52Hs to the 17th BW at Wright-Patterson AFB, phasing down operations at Homestead. On July 25, 1968 the 28th moved, without personnel or aircraft, to Robins AFB replacing the 781st BMS/465th BW. At Robins the 28th flew the B-52G. On October 1, 1983, the 28th was inactivated in conjunction with the 19th BW being redesignated the 19th Air Refueling Wing. The 28th BMS now is assigned to the 384th BW, McConnell AFB, and is equipped with the B-1B.

30th Bombardment Squadron (4133rd SW Grand Forks AFB)—Previously a B-47E squadron in the 19th BW at Homestead, the 30th BMS was assigned to Grand Forks AFB and the 4133rd SW effective January 1, 1962. The unit's first B-52H (61-0015) arrived on April 20, 1962. On February 1, 1963 the 30th was inactivated an replaced by the 46th BMS.

31st Bombardment Squadron (5th BW - Travis AFB; 4126th SW - Beale AFB)—The 31st BMS converted from the B-36 to the B-52G alongside the 23rd BMS at Travis AFB, being fully equipped by June 1, 1959. On October 1, 1959 the 31st was reassigned to the 4126th SW, moving to Beale AFB between November 1959 and January 1960. On August 25, 1961 the unit received SAC's first production GAM-77 Hound Dog missile. On January 9, 1962 the unit conducted the first SAC Combat Evaluation Launch (CEL) of a Hound Dog. The 31st was inactivated on February 1, 1963 when the 4126th was inactivated and replaced by the 456th SAW.

34th Bombardment Squadron (17th BW - Wright-Patterson AFB [H]; Beale AFB [G])—The 34th BMS was activated February 1, 1963 at Wright-Patterson AFB with B-52Es. During June/July 1968 the 34th converted from the B-52E to the B-52H with the first aircraft having arrived from Homestead AFB on April 9, 1968 for familiarization and maintenance training. During the summer of 1975 the 34th was phased down for inactivation. After ceasing alert duty on June 30, 1975 the squadron's last B-52H departed WPAFB on July 7, 1975. On September 30, 1975 the 34th moved, without personnel or aircraft, to Beale AFB replacing the 744th BMS. The 34th flew the B-52G at Beale for exactly one year, inactivating on September 30, 1976.

37th Bombardment Squadron (28th BW - Ellsworth AFB)—The 37th BMS was activated on July 1, 1977 at Ellsworth AFB as part of a reorganization wherein the 28th BW converted from a single squadron of B-52Gs to two squadrons of B-52Hs. The B-52Hs that equipped the squadron were transferred from the 449th and 379th BWs. On October 1, 1982 the 37th was inactivated in another reorganization that saw the 7th and 96th BW retiring the B-52D and converting to the B-52H. The 37th currently is active again in the 28th BW, flying the B-1B.

46th Bombardment Squadron (319th BW - Grand Forks AFB)—The 46th BMS was activated February 1, 1963 at Grand Forks AFB, replacing the 30th BMS/4133rd SW. From 1980 the 46th participated in the Strategic Projection Force with the 23rd at Minot AFB. During the summer of 1982 the 46th converted to the ALCM-capable B-52Gs. The 46th transferred their last B-52G on December 4, 1986, and currently flies the B-1B.

51st Bombardment Squadron (68th BW - Seymour Johnson AFB)—The 51st BMS was activated on April 15, 1963, replacing the 73rd BMS/4241st SW. The 51st exclusively flew the B-52G until the squadron was inactivated on September 30, 1982.

60th Bombardment Squadron (72d BW - Ramey AFB; 43rd SW/43rd BW - Andersen AB)—The 60th BMS converted from B-36s to newly delivered B-52Gs during the second half of 1959, with the first aircraft (58-0168) arriving on August 14, 1959. During the spring of 1971 the 60th phased down for inactivation and the closing of Ramey AFB. On June 30, 1971 the 60th inactivated, but was immediately reactivated at Andersen AB, Guam on July 1, 1971, equipped with the B-52D. During the summer of 1983 the 60th converted to the B-52G once again, adding Harpoon missile capability shortly thereafter. During the spring of 1988 the 60th was released from its nuclear commitments and became a purely conventional squadron. Current with the B-52G/Harpoon. During March 1990 it began phasing down operations for inactivation on June 15, 1990.

62d Bombardment Squadron (39th BW - Eglin AFB; 2d BW - Barksdale AFB)—The 62d BMS was activated on February 1, and assigned to the 39th BW at Eglin AFB. During the 62d's stay at Eglin, test support operations comprised a large portion of the squadron's activities. On June 25, 1965 the 62d moved intact to Barksdale AFB, replacing the 20th Bombardment Squadron and its B-52Fs in the 2d BW. The 62d added OAS and Harpoon capability in the mid-1980s. Current with B-52G/Harpoon.

69th Bombardment Squadron (42d BW - Loring AFB)—The 69th BMS has the distinction of the longest continuous history in the B-52 with the same model, in the same wing, and at the same base. On May 21, 1959 the 69th received its first B-52G (57-6500), and subsequent B-52 deliveries came in two waves: in May/July 1959 and November 1959/January 1961. On March 4, 1972 the 69th received SAC's first production SRAM missile, firing it in an operational test at the White Sands missile range on June 15, 1972. On September 15, 1972 the squadron and wing were declared operational with the SRAM. The 69th also was the first B-52G unit to receive EVS and the Phase VI ECM modifications. After receiving OAS in the mid-1980s and adding Harpoon missile capability, the 69th was released from its nuclear commitment during 1988. Current with B-52G/Harpoon.

70th Bombardment Squadron (42d BW - Loring AFB)—The 70th BMS converted from the B-36 to the B-52G in 1959 alongside the 69th at Loring AFB, but was inactivated on June 25, 1966, transferring its aircraft to the 380th BW at Plattsburgh AFB.

73rd Bombardment Squadron (4241st SW - Seymour Johnson AFB)—The 73rd BMS was activated at Seymour Johnson AFB on January 5, 1959, previously having been a B-36 squadron at Ramey AFB. Their first B-52G (58-0158) arrived on July 24, 1959. This unit was one of the first field units to equip with the Quail decoy missile, flying SAC's first Combat Evaluation Launch of the missile on December 18, 1961. Active in the B-52G for just under four years, the 73rd was inactivated on April 15, 1963 and replaced by the 51st BMS/68th BW.

75th Bombardment Squadron (4039th SW - Griffiss AFB)—The 75th BMS was activated on October 15, 1959 at Griffiss AFB, moving from Loring AFB where it was a B-36 and B-52C/D squadron. The 75th's first B-52G (58-0225) arrived on January 12, 1960. With the February 1, 1963 wave of wing redesignations, the 75th was inactivated and replaced by the 668th BMS/416th BW.

77th Bombardment Squadron (28th BW - Ellsworth AFB)—The 77th BMS, resident at Ellsworth AFB with the 28th BW since the 1940s, converted from the B-52D to the B-52G during 1971. On May 2, 1977 transition to the B-52H began, with the conversion complete on July 20, 1977. In October 1985, the 77th began phasing down B-52H operations for conversion to the B-1B. The 77th currently is a B-1B squadron, still active with the 28th BW at Ellsworth.

93rd Bombardment Squadron (4239th SW - Kinross/Kincheloe AFB)—The 93rd BMS was activated at Kincheloe AFB on August 1, 1961 and assigned to the 4239th SW. On November 8, 1961 its first B-52H (60-0044) was delivered and the squadron became operational shortly thereafter. On February 1, 1963 the 4239th was replaced by the 449th BW, and the 93rd was inactivated.

301st Bombardment Squadron (4135th SW - Eglin AFB)—The 301st BMS was activated at Eglin on June 17, 1959 as part of the 4135th SW and tasked with development and test operations. The squadron's first B-52G (58-0161) was one of the first to be configured for Hound Dog missiles and arrived on July 24, 1959. On February 29, 1960 the squadron participated in the first SAC launch of a Hound Dog missile, followed closely by the first SAC launch of a Quail on June 8, 1960. On September 13, 1960 the squadron received the first production GAM-72s and was the first SAC unit declared operational with the missile on February 1, 1961. On February 1, 1963 the 301st was inactivated and replaced by the 62d BMS/39th BW.

325th Bombardment Squadron (92d SAW/92d BW - Fairchild AFB)—The 325th BMS's history at Fairchild AFB dates back to the B-36 period in the early 1950s. Equipped initially with the B-52C/D from 1956, the 325th converted into the B-52G in January 1971. The 325th was the fourth squadron to equip with ALCM in 1983, and in the summer of 1985 began converting to the B-52H, also with ALCM capability. The first of 19 B-52Hs (60-0032) arrived on September 10, 1985. Current on B-52H/ALCM.

337th Bombardment Squadron (96th BMW, Dyess AFB)—The 337th BMS was formed out of assets of the 39th BMS, shifted to Dyess AFB from Walker AFB on September 15, 1963. Equipped with the B-52E until March 1970 and the B-52D until October 1, 1982, the 337th began conversion to the B-52H with the arrival of the first aircraft on October 1, 1982. The 337th began phasing down in the fall of 1984, transferring its last B-52H to Carswell AFB on January 22, 1985 in preparation for conversion to the B-1B.

340th Bombardment Squadron (97th BMW - Blytheville/Eaker AFB)—The 340th BMS was activated at Blytheville AFB on July 1, 1959 and received its first B-52G (58-0221) on January 9, 1960. The squadron has been continuously operational with B-52Gs since that date, deploying to SEA for "Bullet Shot" in 1972 and becoming the fifth ALCM B-52G squadron in 1984. Current with the B-52G at Eaker AFB.

341st Bombardment Squadron (4038th SW - Dow AFB)—The 341st BMS was activated at Dow AFB on February 15, 1960, having previously been a part of the 97th BMW at Biggs AFB. The squadron's first B-52G (58-0252) arrived on May 27, 1960. The 341st and 4038th SW were inactivated and replaced on February 1, 1963 by the 596th BMS and 397th BW.

342d Bombardment Squadron (4137th SW - Robins) —The 342d BMS also came out of the 97th BMW, and was activated at Robins AFB on May 1, 1960. Its first B-52G (59-2575) arrived on August 4, 1960. Inactivated and replaced on February 1, 1963 by the 765th BMS/465th BW.

441st Bombardment Squadron (320th BW - Mather AFB)—The 441st BMS was activated at Mather AFB on February 1, 1963, and operated the B-52F until the summer of 1968. As the 23rd Bombardment Squadron at Travis AFB drew down, the 441st built up in the B-52G. The 441st participated in "Bullet Shot" combat operations in 1972. On October 1, 1988 the 441st was relived of its nuclear commitments and became a purely conventional unit. On July 1, 1989 the squadron began phasing down for inactivation on September 30, 1989.

524th Bombardment Squadron (379th BW - Wurtsmith AFB)—The 524th BMS moved to Wurtsmith AFB on January 9, 1961 and became SAC's first B-52H squadron with the arrival of 60-0001 on May 9, 1961. Operational with the B-52H through June 1977. Converted to the B-52G in a 'swap' with the 28th BW at Ellsworth AFB. Second squadron to add ALCM capability in 1982. Added full external/internal conventional capability in 1988. Current with B-52G.

525th Bombardment Squadron (4136th SW - Minot AFB)—Previously a B-47 squadron at Homestead AFB, the 525th BMS was activated at Minot AFB on March 15, 1961. Delivery of the squadron's first B-52H (60-0025) occurred on July 13, 1961. The 525th and 4136th were inactivated on February 1, 1963 and replaced by the 720th BMS and 450th BW.

526th Bombardment Squadron (4024th SW - K. I. Sawyer AFB)—Also a Homestead AFB B-47 squadron, the 526th BMS activated at K. I. Sawyer AFB on June 1, 1961. The first B-52H (60-0024) arrived on July 31, 1961. Inactivated on February 1, 1963 and replaced by the 644th BMS/410th BW.

528th Bombardment Squadron (380th SAW, Plattsburgh AFB)—Standing down from B-47 operations at Plattsburgh AFB in the spring of 1966, the 528th BMS was redesignated from Medium to Heavy and commenced B-52G operations on June 25, 1966. The crews and aircraft assigned to the squadron were transferred from the 70th BMS at Loring AFB. On January 5, 1971, the 528th transferred its last B-52G to Fairchild AFB and began preparation for conversion to the FB-111A. Current with FB-111A at Plattsburgh.

596th Bombardment Squadron (397th BW - Dow AFB; 2d BW - Barksdale AFB)—The 596th BMS was activated February 1, 1963 at Dow AFB, replacing the 341st BS. Remaining in the B-52G, the 596th moved intact to Barksdale AFB during the summer of 1969, officially joining the 2nd BW on April 25, 1968. Added ALCM capability in late 1985/early 1986, receiving modified B-52Gs from Fairchild AFB. Current on B-52G at Barksdale AFB.

644th Bombardment Squadron (410th BW, K. I. Sawyer AFB)—Activated at K. I. Sawyer AFB on February 1, 1963, the 644th BMS replaced the 526th BMS/4042d SW. The 644th has flown the B-52H continuously since that date, and was the first B-52H unit to equip with the SRAM, EVS, and the Phase VI ECM package. From 1987, the squadron added the AN/ALQ-172 ECM system and advanced cruise missile integration(ACMI), though the AGM-129A ACM itself is not yet operational with the unit. Current with the B-52H.

668th Bombardment Squadron (416th BW - Griffiss AFB)—Activated on February 1, 1963 at Griffiss AFB, replacing the 75th BMS and inheriting the 75th's personnel and B-52Gs. Griffiss received its first AGM-86B ALCM on January 11, 1981 with the first production model arriving at the base on April 23. On August 15, 1981, the first B-52G (58-0247) modified with OAS and cruise missile integration (CMI) joined the unit. Just over one year later, the 668th participated in the first launch of an ALCM from an operational unit. The 668th's ALCM conversion activities culminated in placing ALCM on alert on December 16, 1982. Added full external/internal conventional capability during 1988. Current on B-52G.

716th Bombardment Squadron (449th BW - Kinross/Kincheloe AFB)—Replaced the 93rd BMS at Kincheloe AFB on February 1, 1963. Operated B-52Hs into the summer of 1977. Began transferring aircraft to the 28th BW at Ellsworth AFB in June, with the last B-52H departing Kincheloe on July 20, 1977. The squadron and the 449th BW were inactivated on September 30, 1977, marking the closure of Kincheloe AFB, Michigan.

720th Bombardment Squadron (450th BW - Minot AFB)—Activated on February 1, 1963 at Minot AFB, taking over for the 525th BMS/4136th SW. Operated the B-52H until replaced by the 23rd BMS/5th BW on July 25, 1968.

744th Bombardment Squadron (456th SAW/456th BW - Beale AFB)—Activated on February 1, 1963 at Beale AFB, assuming the role of the 31st BMS. Operated B-52Gs from Beale and deployed as part of the "Bullet Shot" missions to Andersen AB in 1972. Inactivated on September 30, 1975 and replaced by the 34th BMS/17th BW.

781st Bombardment Squadron (465th BW - Robins AFB)—Activated at Robins AFB on February 1, 1963, the 781st BMS flew the B-52 until it was replaced by the 28th BMS/19th BW on July 25, 1968.

CONSTRUCTION AND SYSTEMS:

The Boeing B-52 *Stratofortress* is a land-based heavy bombardment aircraft. The aircraft is characterized by swept wings and tail surfaces, four underslung nacelles housing eight jet engines, a quadricycle main landing gear and a tip gear near each outboard engine nacelle, just inboard of each external fuel tank.

COCKPIT

The crew compartment is located in the extreme forward fuselage and is divided into an upper and lower deck. The pilots' stations are located at the forward end of the upper deck while the electronic warfare officer (EWO) and gunner have aft-facing seats on the aft end of the upper deck. The radar-navigator's and navigator's stations are on the lower deck forward of the main entry door. In addition to the basic six-man crew, the following crew members are provided for: an instructor pilot seated between and immediately aft of the pilots, a defense instructor seated on the right side of the upper deck ahead of the EWO facing aft, and an instructor navigator seated at the aft end of the lower deck for takeoff and landing or on a removable seat between and immediately aft of the navigators for instructing. Provisions for a "tenth man" are provided by using the oxygen fittings and interphone panel near the bunk on the B-52H and by the ditching seat behind the IP seat in the B-52G. The crew compartment extends from a pressure bulkhead forward of the pilots' stations to a pressure bulkhead aft of the EWO's and gunner's stations. The interior of the crew compartment is painted light grey.

Food storage boxes are located in the general vicinity of each seat. Three electrically powered "hot cups" are provided, one near each pair of seats, along with a single two-gallon water container. The B-52 is equipped with a toilet (it doubles as the defense instructor's seat) located directly forward of the EWO's seat. A mattress is stowed directly behind the pilot's seat on the B-52G and is placed in the aisle between the right and left electronics racks when used. Fittings are provided in the floor of the aisle for use of a safety belt. A crew bunk is provided on the B-52H directly aft of the pilot's seat, underneath the left load central circuit breaker panel. It is equipped with an oxygen regulator, interphone panel, safety belt and a reading light.

Movement of the flight crew between the decks is facilitated by a five-step ladder forward of the main entry door. Movement through the equipment area, forward wheel well, bomb bay, aft wheel well and aft equipment compartment is possible during flight via a crawlway on the right side of the fuselage. Access to the unpressurized portion of the fuselage is not generally required for normal flight operations.

The pilots are the only crewmembers on the B-52G/H provided with windows. Window numbering begins with the No. 1 window (the center windscreen) wrapping around each side with 2L and 2R (pilot's and copilot's windscreens) and 3, 4 and 5 L and R respectively. The small "eyebrow" windows, especially useful during air refueling, are numbered 6L and 6R. In addition there is a window in each pilot's escape hatch that provides a measure of visibility directly upward. All windows except 6L and 6R are constructed of inner and outer laminated tempered glass panes with a vinyl core between the panes. The two "eyebrow" windows (6L and 6R) are acrylic plastic. The pilot's and copilot's sliding windows (the forward most of the three side windows - 3L and 3R) may be opened or closed as required while on the ground. A conductive film is located next to the vinyl core for window defog/anti-icing. Windows 1 through 4L/4R have window anti-ice, which heats the outer pane, while windows 5L/5R and the escape hatch windows have window defog, which heats the inner pane. Four-speed windshield wipers are fitted to the forward windscreen in front of the pilot and copilot.

Upward firing ejection seats are provided for the four crewmembers on the upper deck, while downward firing seats are provided for the two crewmembers on the lower deck. Provisions are made in both types of seats to accommodate a survival kit and back-type automatic opening parachute and integrated harness. Each seat can be positioned electrically up and down, fore and aft, and tilted. The upward seats are equipped with folding armrests which contain arming levers used to prepare the seat for ejection. The downward firing seats have an ejection control trigger ring stowed on the front center of the seat. A series of ballistic devices and mechanical linkages incorporated into the seat will lock the inertia reel, stow the control column (pilots), writing table (navigators), or fire-control pedestal (gunner), jettison the hatch and arm the seat for ejection. An alarm system will signal ABANDON when either the pilot's or copilot's control column stows. Additionally, there is a three-position guarded switch on the aisle stand providing a bailout warning (flashing) and abandon (steady) light.

A three-section catapult is incorporated to eject each seat from the aircraft, and is fired by squeezing either of the firing triggers located inside of each arming lever (upward seats) or continuing to pull the trigger ring (downward seats). Each seat is equipped with a headrest and inertia reel which assist the occupant in maintaining position during ejection. The downward seats also have leg guards and ankle restraints. An integrated harness release mechanism provides a means for separating the safety belt and parachute harness from the seat automatically after ejection. A modified B-5 parachute and a specially designed manual safety belt are installed in the harness release fittings. A zero delay lanyard provides for an improved low-altitude escape capability.

The aircraft is provided with a 300 psi liquid oxygen system to supply all crew stations and the portable oxygen bottle rechargers. The system is supplied by three

B-52H, 60-0001, initially was delivered to Wurtsmith AFB, Michigan, on 9 May 1961. It was assigned to the 28th BW, Ellsworth AFB, SD, in this October, 1985 photo.

B-52H, 60-0002, of 7th BW on final approach to Carswell AFB in 1985. TF33 auxiliary inlet doors are seen in typically variable positions with the aircraft at traffic pattern airspeeds.

B-52H, 60-0003, 7th BW, named "Master Blaster", taxis in at Carswell with 12 AGM-86B ALCMs. Open inlet doors indicate only inboard engines are running.

B-52H, 60-0004, of 410th BW, taxis at K. I. Sawyer AFB, Michigan on September 8, 1986. Wing patch on nose is in low visibility blue and gray.

JB-52H, 60-0006, inflight near Edwards AFB, California in early 1960's. Dayglo orange panels are added to standard "bare metal" scheme.

B-52H-135-BW, 60-0007, of the 7th BW at Carswell with training load of 12 external ACM-86B ALCMs. Standard Strategic paint scheme.

25-liter 300 psi liquid oxygen converters located in the aft equipment compartment and the system can provide a crew of six with up to 70+ hours of breathable oxygen.

FUSELAGE

The semi-monocoque fuselage has a rectangular cross-section built around four longerons with closely-spaced circumferential frames. It is 9 ft. 10 in. wide and 12 ft. 1.4 in. high. The fuselage contains the pressurized crew compartment, a bomb bay, and four main wheel wells located two forward of and two aft of the bomb bay.

Four major subassemblies form the fuselage. They include the forward fuselage (section 41), the mid-fuselage containing the bomb bay, wheel wells and body fuel tanks (section 43), the aft fuselage section containing miscellaneous equipment and the strike camera (section 47) and the tail section containing ECM equipment and the tail turret (section 49).

A 32.5 in. wide and 31.4 in. long main entry door located on the belly centerline is provided for access to the lower deck of the crew compartment. It is hinged on the forward edge, opens downward approximately 75 ft. and is 4 ft. 4.3 in. from the ground. This is a change from first-generation B-52s where the door was hinged on the aft edge and not located on the centerline. The door is supported in its open position by two cables, which also keep the door from opening too quickly. An entrance ladder is installed on the inner side of the door.

Six escape hatches are provided that form a part of the airframe structure when closed. They are located directly above the four crewmembers seated on the upper deck, and directly below the crewmembers seated on the lower deck. The EWO, gunner, and two navigators' hatches are equipped with aerodynamic hatch lifters that ensure proper hatch separation during the automatic ejection sequence. The upper four hatches also may be manually jettisoned for use during ditching or ground accidents.

A 28 ft. long, 6 ft. wide bomb bay is located in the fuselage directly beneath the wing. The bomb door system comprises six double-panel doors which cover the bomb bay. All actuation occurs on the lower panels only, the upper panels are hinged to provide a larger opening for ground service. The doors are latched at the forward and aft bulkheads of the bomb bay. To secure simultaneous action of all doors, the center doors are mechanically linked to the forward and aft doors. The doors can be operated with the bomb door switch on either the pilot's or radar-navigator's control panel and the OAS and AGM-69A systems can operate the doors automatically. The conventional munitions modifications (TOs 1B-52G-777 and 1B-52H-702) provided structural modifications to the aft wall area of the bomb bay to permit release of internal high-drag munitions throughout the flight envelope, from all stations.

The one-piece nose radome is constructed of honeycomb core and glass fiber outer layers bonded together with synthetic resins. The radome is hinged along the upper aft surface and swings upward. The nose radome is protected from lightning by diverter strips, and is covered by a coating of anti-rain/erosion finish. A flush-fitting Doppler radome is located in the bottom fuselage just aft of the forward landing gear. A bulged AFSATCOM radome is installed just aft of the EWO and gunner's escape hatches on the top of the fuselage centerline. A retractable ECM radome is located just aft of the drag chute door. The radome is constructed of reinforced fiberglass with a honeycomb core and retracts to prevent damage during drag chute deployment. Various other communication and ECM radomes, mostly constructed of fiberglass, are located around the aircraft, mainly on the nose and tail sections.

WINGS

The wing of the B-52 was a major departure from the earlier B-47 style wing. The increased thickness of the wing structure permitted the installation of fuel tanks which greatly improved the span loading characteristics[9]. The additional fuel and the high aspect ratio (8.55:1) also improved the range of the aircraft. The wing is swept 35 ft. at quarter-chord. The chord at the root is 30 ft. 11 in. and 12 ft. 4 in. at the tip. Installation of the wing is at a 6′ angle of incidence to the fuselage with a 2.5 ft. dihedral. The wing uses Boeing proprietary airfoils, labeled BAC-233 at the root and BAC-236 at the tip. It is attached to the fuselage with bottle-shaped hollow terminal pins.

Five major sections comprise the wing: a center section, two inboard sections and two outboard sections. The wing's main component is the box-shaped center section constructed from front and rear spars with machine tapered upper and lower skin surfaces supported and strengthened by inspar ribs (running from leading to trailing edge) and stiffeners (from wingtip to wingtip). The rear spar is heavier than the front since it absorbs greater aerodynamic loads. The entire portion of the wing between the forward and aft spars is occupied by fuel. Flight controls are mounted along the aft spar of the inboard wing panels, and spoilers are located on the upper surface of the outboard wing panels. The fixed portions of the wing trailing edge are permanently attached to the wing rear spar and consist of aluminum ribs and beams covered with either aluminum or stiffened and bonded magnesium skin panels.

The engine thrust loads are transmitted to the wing by three beams which form the main structural components of the engine nacelle struts. The engines are supported from the strut by a firewall constructed of titanium alloy. Panels on the sides of the struts permit access to engine electrical wiring, plumbing and throttle control cables.

The wing leading edge sections are constructed as D-shaped sections with widely spaced ribs attached to spar angles at their upper and lower aft edges. Each section is fastened to the wing with bolts through the front spar caps and the spar angles. Strakelets were added to ALCM-capable B-52Gs at the juncture of the wing leading edge and the fuselage as part of the unratified SALT II treaty, which required a method of visually identifying what bombers were cruise-missile equipped. The strakelets show up particularly well in satellite photos. These devices also improve the airflow, resulting in approximately a two percent improvement in aerodynamic efficiency. The wingtips are fabricated of fiberglass and contain antenna for various ECM systems.

Fifty vortex generators are installed on the wing upper surfaces between the inboard engine pylon and the fuselage, a change from the arrangement used by the first-generation B-52s. Aircraft equipped for launching ALCMs (both B-52Gs and B-52Hs) have another 31 vortex generators installed along the upper surface of the wing just aft of the leading edge straddling the weapons pylon.

Four-section Fowler-type flaps are located on the trailing wing surface and provide 797 sq. ft. of surface. The flaps are constructed of aluminum alloy frames with bonded aluminum alloy skins. During the first 37.5 ft. of extension, the flaps rotate downward 35 ft. with little rearward movement. For the remainder of the extension, the flaps move rearward only. Most of the drag occurs during the first 20% of flap motion. This initial 20% rotates the flaps down 29 ft. in approximately 12 sec., leaving only 6 ft. of rotation in the remaining 80% of flap extension. A pair of 205 Volt, three-phase ac motors, joined by differential gearing, make up the flap power unit which is located in the fuselage aft of the rear wing spar. The flap power unit drives a set of torque tubes, which in turn rotate a pair of flap drive gears which turn a jack-screw in each flap.

Seven hydraulically actuated spoiler segments are located on the upper surface of each wing. The spoilers can operate symmetrically when serving as airbrakes, and differentially for lateral control. The four outboard spoilers are mechanically linked to operate as a unit, as are the three inboard sections. The spoilers have a maximum deflection of 60 ft., though in AIRBRAKE mode, the outboard spoiler groups only go to 50 ft.

Another change from first-generation B-52s was the replacement of the jettisonable 3,000 gal. external fuel

---
[9] The development of this "thick" wing, as opposed to the B-47s thin wing, allowed stowage of equipment (fuel or landing gear) in the wing itself. This would be the breakthrough needed by Boeing to proceed with the development of the first truly successful jet transport, the model 707/717 series.

tanks with fixed 700 gal. tanks. These tanks are located near each wing tip, and serve to stabilize the wing against flutter.

TAIL SURFACES

In planform and area (900 sq. ft.) the horizontal stabilizers of all B-52s are identical. The stabilizer spans 52 ft., has a root chord of 27 ft. 8.3 in. and a tip chord of 6 ft. 11 in. Sweepback at quarter-chord is 35 ft. and it has zero degrees of dihedral. The stabilizer is comprised of the center section and two outboard sections. The center section (torque box) passes through the fuselage and is a box beam made up of an auxiliary spar (front) and a main spar (rear). The outboard sections are of monospar construction with the leading and trailing edge sections attached to ribs cantilevered from the monospar. A 79 sq. ft. elevator is installed on each stabilizer. The B-52G and B-52H do not have the trim tabs installed on the first-generation B-52s. The elevators are constructed of aluminum alloy frames with flush-riveted aluminum alloy skins.

Each horizontal stabilizer has 35 vortex generators on both the upper and lower surfaces so as to increase elevator authority by controlling the boundary layer air. The entire horizontal stabilizer is designed to pivot 4 ft. down and 9 ft. up from the aircraft waterline to provide trim control. This has resulted in several incidents when pilots took off with the stabilizer in an incorrect position since the elevator does not have enough authority to completely overcome stabilizer trim. The leading edge of the stabilizer is raised or lowered by a jackscrew driven by two hydraulic motors, one driving the screw, the other driving the nut.

The vertical stabilizer of the B-52G/H was a radical departure from the earlier models, being 91 in. shorter with a full length rudder. The vertical fin is 22 ft. 11 in. high and the sweep at quarter-chord is 35 ft. It has a maximum chord of 25 ft. 2 in. and the chord at the tip is 10 ft. The fin incorporates a single main spar and auxiliary spars forward and aft. The rudder is an aluminum alloy frame covered with flush-riveted aluminum skin, hinged to the aft auxiliary spar in six places. The vertical stabilizer folds at the fuselage juncture to permit certain maintenance and to allow storage of the aircraft in comparatively low hangars. Fiberglass fairings were added on each side of the vertical stabilizer when the AN/ALQ-153 tail warning radar was installed.

The aerodynamically balanced rudder and elevators are fitted with actuators that receive both mechanical and electrical inputs. The mechanical inputs come from the pilot's control wheel and rudder pedals, while the electrical signals are generated by the stability augmentation system (SAS). The maximum elevator deflection is "19" for mechanical control inputs, and "10" in yaw and "5" in pitch for SAS inputs. Two elevator actuators are incorporated in the pitch axis control system to provide an irreversible actuation system. Elevator feel and centering is provided by an elevator Q-spring in the cable system. Pilot effort required to maneuver the aircraft is increased at low airspeeds (providing trim stimulus) and decreased at high airspeeds (providing improved maneuvering capabilities), with positive centering at all airspeeds (increasing trim stability).

LANDING GEAR

The landing gear on the B-52 is composed of four main gears and two tip protection gears. The landing gear are electrically controlled, hydraulically actuated, and mechanically locked. The dual wheel main landing gears are in a unique quadricycle arrangement with two side-by-side forward gears and two side-by-side rear gears. The tip protection gear are located between the outboard engine strut and the external fuel tank and support the wing under high gross weight loading conditions and also provides shock cushion during take off, taxi and landing. The landing gear is fully retracted in 10 to 15 seconds or extended in 15 to 20 seconds.

The tip protection gear well is aft of the wing rear spar and is trapezoid in shape, measuring 115.8 x 30.0 x 39.5 in. A 20 x 4.4 tubed tire is mounted on each tip protection gear wheel. The tip gear doors are in two sections, with the strut section connected to the tip gear and following the cycle of operation of the gear. The wheel well section is hydraulically actuated and is controlled for proper sequence operation by mechanical linkage in the tip gear system.

Fuselage bulkheads at stations 538 and 1135 (the zero datum is located 32 in. forward of the nose) afford mounting provisions for the main gear struts. The gear assumes a vertical position when extended. The left gear

B-52H-135-BW, 60-0008, inflight over Georgia in August 1988. Nose down body angle-of-attack is typical at most cruise speeds and gross weights. Crew name "Box" is in shape of Texas map.

B-52H-135-BW, 60-0009, of 7th BW at Carswell. "Balls 9" was first "flagship" of 9th Bomb Sq. Enlarged "9" and "BMS" markings were unique to the 9th and designed by co-author Rogers.

retract forward, up and inboard, the right gear retract aft, up and inboard. Retraction and extension are accomplished by the drag strut, hydraulic actuator and eccentric shaft. The wheel doors are controlled mechanically. Door actuators hold the doors open when the gear is extended. Each main gear strut has two aluminum wheels which accommodate 56 x 16 38-ply tubeless tires, although 32-ply tires were initially used.

The steering system permits either ground steering or crosswind landing, depending upon the pilot's selection. In the steering mode, maximum authority is ±55° of center during taxiing and ±12° during take off and landing. In the steering mode only the forward gear move. When crosswind is selected, all four main gear may traverse up to 20° to either side of center. When the gear are in a crosswind position, they automatically center before retraction. Safety switches are incorporated in the main gear that detect when the oleo struts are compressed, indicating the aircraft is on the ground. When this is true, the chaff and flare dispensers are disabled, most anti-ice systems become inoperative, avionics ground cooling systems blowers are activated and the flight loads data recorder is turned off.

Bendix segmented rotor-type brakes are installed on all eight main gear wheels. The brakes on all wheels are identical. An anti-skid system is fitted, although unlike more modern systems it is not capable of modulating braking effort, instead it simply "turns on" or "turns off" the brakes in response to excessive rotational deceleration. A 44-foot diameter ribbon parachute is used to augment the braking system. The parachute is installed in a compartment aft of the rudder in the top of the tail section. It theoretically is possible to land the aircraft with any two of the four main gear extended, as long as at least one of the extended gear is forward.

HYDRAULIC SYSTEM

The landing gear, brakes, steering, spoilers, rotary launcher, elevators, rudder, horizontal stabilizer, bomb bay doors and inflight refueling doors are all actuated hydraulically.

The hydraulic system of the B-52 differs from a conventional system in decentralization. Instead of the usual single main system, there are six independent engine-driven systems consisting of inboard and outboard right and left wing hydraulic systems and right and left body hydraulic systems. The engine-driven systems, which supply normal pressure to the wing and body systems, are mounted on the right side of engines 1, 3, 4, 5, 6, and 7. In addition, there are two electric motor-driven primary hydraulic systems, which supply normal pressure to the No.1 and 2 rudder/elevator hydraulic systems, and are mounted on the right side of the aft fuselage. Electric motor-driven standby pumps, available for use in all systems except the inboard wing systems, are installed at the left and right wing trailing edge locations and left and right body locations. Additionally there is an electric motor-driven pump on the left side of the bomb bay to provide hydraulic power to rotate the SRAM launcher or CSRL. It normally is connected to the No. 4 (left body) hydraulic system but can be operated from the No. 5 (right body) system via a three-position switch on the pilot's hydraulic control panel.

The engine-driven pumps have a rated flow of 12 gallons per minute at an output pressure of 2,800 psi, with a cutout pressure of 3,000 psi. Each electric motor-driven standby pump has a rated flow of 3 gallons per minute at 1,300 rpm. Oil-air type accumulators are incorporated to provide air preload pressure for accelerating the operation of outboard wing system components and certain body system components.

ELECTRICAL SYSTEMS

Primary and secondary electrical distribution buses supply power to the aircraft. Primary power is supplied by four engine-driven generators (70/90 KVA on B-52G, 120 KVA on B-52H) and constant speed drives mounted on engines 1, 3, 5 and 7. The constant speed drives maintain each generator at 6,000 rpm to produce the desired constant frequency (400 Hz). This 118/205 volt three-phase ac power is used for most heavy loads such as boost pumps and wing flap motors. Single-phase 118 volt ac power is used for small motors, actuators, heating and some electronic equipment.

Primary dc power is produced by eight transformer-rectifier (TR) units which receive 205 volt ac, step it down and rectify it to 28 vdc. Of the eight TR units, three power the aft dc system and are located in the aft fuselage. The

B-52H-135-BW, 60-0010, of 7th BW in SIOP scheme with "toned down" dark gray nose. Other markings are standard for type and period (1985).

B-52H-135-BW, 60-0011, of 7th BW at Carswell on Oct. 6, 1988. External load of AFM-86B ALCMs and pylons impart significant forward CG moment. ALCM fuel load and sequence is designed to compensate.

B-52 CAPABILITY COMPARISON

	B-52D	B-52G	B-52H
Range – N Mi (High Altitude, Internal Payload)	6,400	7,300	8,800
Speed – KTAS	530	550	545
Combat Ceiling – Feet	45,000	46,000	47,000
Offensive Weapons – Max Quantity			
Gravity – Conventional	108	27	27
Gravity – Nuclear	4	8	8
Missile (SRAM) – Nuclear	0	20	20
Active Defense Weapons – Quantity and Type	4 .50 Cal Guns MD-9 FCS	4 .50 Cal Guns ASG-15 FCS	1 20mm Gun ASG-21 FCS
Passive Defense System – Quantity and Type			
Chaff	1125 Pkgs ALE-27	1125 Pkgs ALE-24	1125 Pkgs ALE-24
Flares	96 ALE-20	192 ALE-20	192 ALE-20
ECM – Type	Phase V	Phase VI	Phase VI
Low Level Capability – Feet	500	300	300
Terrain Avoidance Radar – Type	ASQ-48	ASQ-151	ASQ-151

remaining five TR units power the forward dc system and are located in the right forward wheel well. Two batteries located in the forward wheel wells provide an auxiliary source of 24 vdc power which is supplied to essential and emergency equipment in case of total power failure. A separate nickel-cadmium battery is installed to provide power for the special weapons emergency release system (SWESS). Aircraft ac and dc power is also provided to weapons in the bomb bay and suspended on the wing pylons. Three external power receptacles are provided for energizing aircraft equipment from an external source: a main receptacle located on the right side of the fuselage adjacent to the forward wheel well; a bombing navigational system receptacle located immediately aft of the main external receptacle; and a fire control system receptacle located aft and adjacent to the right rear wheel well.

MISCELLANEOUS SYSTEMS

The bleed air system incorporates a wing leading edge manifold and controls for collecting and routing high pressure hot air. This air may be obtained either from the final stage compressor of each operating engine, or from an auxiliary air source applied to a ground start connection on the underside of each nacelle. The bleed air system is the power source for engine starting and the air source for heating, cooling and pressurizing the crew compartment. The system is designed so that normal airflow is from the No. 2 nacelle through a ram air heat exchanger (precooler) in the No. 2 strut into distribution ducting in the wing leading edge and fuselage. In flight, the heat exchanger keeps duct air temperature at or below 190°C. In the event of failure of the bleed air supply from the No. 2 nacelle, emergency airflow may be obtained from the No. 3 nacelle, although use of this source of bleed air is only recommended at altitudes above 25,000 ft. Recent modifications have changed some plumbing and added additional controls.

The air conditioning system provides crew compartment ventilation and pressurization, piped cooling to electronic equipment, and emergency ram air ventilation. High pressure hot air from the bleed air system provides the energy to air condition and pressurize the crew compartment utilizing the equivalent of approximately six percent of thrust output of one engine. The air conditioning pack located just aft of the crew compartment cools the hot bleed air by means of two air-to-air heat exchangers and an air cycle machine. The cold air supply is divided between crew and equipment cooling so the crew will receive up to 75% of the cold air output. Cabin pressure is regulated by controlling the outflow of air from the cabin. A retractable ram airscoop is located on the left side of the fuselage to provide an emergency source of ram air for cooling and ventilating the crew compartment. The scoop will automatically cyclically extend and retract to prevent ice buildup.

A fixed landing light is installed on each forward landing gear door for use during approach and landing. Navigation lights consist of a red light on the left wingtip, a green light on the right wingtip, two white lights on the tip of each horizontal stabilizer, a white light on the top of the fuselage, and a white light on each side of the fuselage above the bomb bay doors. Three rotating anti-collision lights are provided, one on each side of the fuselage and one on the bottom of the fuselage. A crosswind landing light is installed on the right forward landing gear to provide lighting during crosswind landing. A retractable terrain clearance light is installed on the forward bottom fuselage to provide illumination during a night crash landing. Three taxi lights, one installed on the leading edge of each wing just outboard of the outboard engine nacelles, and one on the right forward landing gear, and the crosswind landing light provide lighting for taxi operations. Air refueling lights consist of five white lights, one installed in the receptacle and two in each slipway door. The lights illuminate the receptacle, slipway, and wing areas during night air refueling operations. The lights in the slipway doors may also be used for scanning the wing leading edges, nacelles, struts and spoilers.

A stability augmentation system (SAS) is installed in the aircraft to substantially reduce structural fatigue damage rates and peak loads, to improve Dutch Roll damping, and to improve the controllability of the aircraft under turbulent flight conditions. The SAS is an electrohydraulic two-axis (pitch and yaw) system which replaced the original magnetic and electromechanical yaw dampers. The system uses three hydraulic actuators; one for the rudder and two for the elevators.

CAMERA SYSTEMS

The B-52 is equipped with both a strike camera system and a bombing-navigational system camera. The strike camera system is used for taking strike and recon-

B-52H-165-BW, 61-012, of 7th BW landing at Carswell. View from almost directly below shows TF33 engine cowl shape to great advantage.

B-52G, 57-6497, on Boeing, Wichita delivery ramp freshly painted in the SIOP camouflage scheme. Pylons for the AN/ALE-25 chaff rocket pods are installed between the engine nacelle pylons but the dispensers are not.

B-52G, (serial number unknown), on Boeing, Wichita delivery ramp freshly painted in a SIOP scheme variation. Appearing to be a reversal pattern, it was tested but never adopted for use. Colors appear to be the same as conventional SIOP colors.

Early **B-52H,** (serial number unknown), in natural metal/white scheme with "Hound Dog" missile. These markings were standard during the first few years of B-52G/H service. Slight airbrake/spoiler extension is visible.

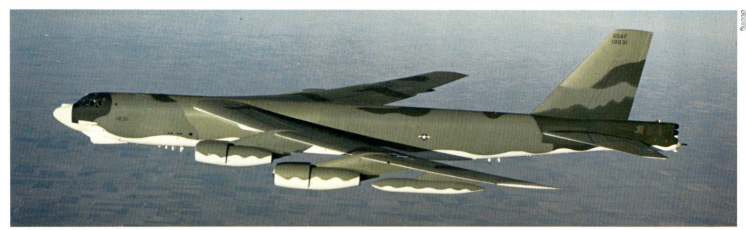

B-52H-170-BW, 61-031, during pre-delivery flight test near Boeing's Wichita facility. This aircraft is believed to have been the first EVS/Phase VI B-52H conversion. AN/AW-155 antennas under forward fuselage are evident.

B-52H-135-BW, 60-0006, at Edwards AFB. This aircraft was part of the Air Force Flight Test Center test fleet during 1963 time frame. Slightly faded day-glo orange on forward fuselage, fin, engine nacelles, and wing leading edges.

Douglas GAM-87 "Skybolt" being moved into position under a test B-52G wing support pylon assembly. Inverted "Y" pylon could accommodate two "Skybolts". One pylon was suspended under each wing root section. "Skybolt" normally would have been nuclear warhead equipped.

B-52G, 58-0189, of 379th BW in England for the 1980 "Great Strike" competition. "Triangle K" was the 379th BG's tail marking during WWII and was in gunship gray and black. The same tail marking is visible still on current 379th BW B-52Gs.

B-52G, 58-0206, of 43rd BW visiting Australia on May 9, 1984. SIOP paint scheme was slightly faded and the nose radome had not yet been toned down as per updated, second generation markings. Shortly afterwards aircraft was painted in gray-on-gray scheme.

B-52G, 58-0226, at Pease AFB, N.H. on June 27, 1975. Aircraft has fresh SIOP paint but is pre-EVS and pre-Phase VI update. Distinct scalloping of white undersurface paint is indicative of early camouflage scheme.

B-52G, 58-0222, of the 92nd BW, during May 1985, had the dark gray radome but white EVS turret. The latter betrayed the fact that the forward fuselage did not yet have "wrap-around" paint. Modified wing root fairings are readily discernible from this vantage point.

B-52G, 58-0240, of the 2nd BW transient at Carswell AFB on October 30, 1984. Red map of Louisiana, "2nd", and star indicate this aircraft was one of Barksdale's bombing competition entries. "Four-tone" camouflage is noteworthy.

"Conventional" *B-52G, 58-0242*, of the 93rd BW, at Castle AFB on October 18, 1987. "Strategic" camouflage is F.S. 36081 Gray/F.S. 34086 Green on top and sides. Lack of "pop-up" antenna aft of drag chute door indicates this aircraft has AN/ALQ-172 ECM.

B-52H-140-BW, 60-0014, on final to Carswell AFB. Nose radome was painted in the dark gray but "tone-down" wrap-around gray on nose was not yet applied.

B-52H-170-BW, 61-016, of 7th BW at Carswell undergoes minor maintenance with nose radome and various engine cowlings open. Photo date was July 5, 1985.

B-52H-140-BW, 60-0017, 7th BW, on final approach to Carswell AFB in 1984. Extended aft fuselage associated with Phase VI ECM mod is clearly evident.

Undated photo of B-52H-140-BW, 60-0018, shows the B-52H before the addition of EVS turrets and Phase VI ECM protuberances. Note gray underwing panels.

naissance photographs from high altitude. An electrically operated camera door protects the camera when it is not in operation. The engine bleed system provides heating air to the insulated camera compartment, and also provides air for the vacuum system which holds the film in place during exposure. The strike camera system has used type K-17C, K-17D and K-38 cameras. Camera control is provided by an intervalometer located at the radar-navigator's station.

Initially the B-52G was equipped with a type O-32 bombing navigational system camera. Subsequently, the B-52Gs and B-52Hs were equipped with a type KS-32A camera for use with the AN/ASB-9A and AN/ASB-16 bombing navigation systems. With the incorporation of OAS in 1982, an RO-523/ASQ-175 video recorder was installed in lieu of the KS-32A.

AVIONICS

As originally installed in the B-52H, and retrofitted to the B-52G, the advanced capability radar (ACR) provided for terrain avoidance (TA), and included some anti-jamming and low-level mapping capabilities. The ACR gave three dimensional information on three five-inch CRTs located in front of the pilot, copilot and navigator. Information displayed on the CRTs included the aircraft's range from a given point, its elevation and azimuth. The height of the terrain around the aircraft also was shown continuously at selected distances of three, six or ten miles from the aircraft. The ACR presentations took one of two different forms. In the PLAN mode, the presentation was map-like, and showed how the terrain was configured ±60° from the ground track of the aircraft, out to a range of ten miles. In the PROFILE mode, the presentation was a vertical one, and showed the track ±45° in azimuth and 1,500 ft. in elevation. The display was a silhouette of the terrain in front of the aircraft, with the highest projection at any azimuth angle displayed.

The ACR antenna was located in the extreme nose of the aircraft, and rotated 360° at either 8.5 rpm (slow mode) or 20 rpm (fast). It could also operate in a sector scan configuration, sweeping back and forth with a scan width varying from 15 to 220° depending on mode. The antenna reflector tilted manually from 3.5° upward to 32° downward with the normal operational position being from 6 to 13° down. The advanced capability radar was retained in a modified form, although the original round TA scopes were deleted. The radar image was presented on the navigators' multifunction displays and also on the pilots' EVS monitors as a terrain trace during TA operations. (The TA display was incorporated into EVS when EVS was installed in the 1970's—prior to OAS mod.)

As originally delivered, the B-52G/H were equipped with the AN/ASQ-38(V) bombing navigational integrated system (BNS), which consisted of: MD-1 automatic astrocompass; AN/AJA-1 or AN/AJN-8 true heading computer system; AN/APN-89A Doppler radar; and an AN/ASB-9A or AN/ASB-16 bombing-navigational system. The BNS was designed to be highly automatic in operation by interconnection of the various systems. The Doppler radar system fed ground speed and drift data to the AN/ASB-16, which in turn supplied data to the other BNS components. Latitude and longitude data was supplied to the true heading computer and to the automatic astrocompass system. The bombing-navigation system could also be operated independently from the rest of the BNS.

An update of the bombing-navigation system was initiated for the B-52G/H starting in 1980. This new digital (instead of analog), solid-state system provided more accurate navigation, position fix and weapons delivery capabilities, as well as substantially increased reliability. The original AN/ASQ-38(V) bombing-navigation system was replaced by a new AN/ASQ-176 offensive avionics system (OAS) equipped with a digital computer, although some of the old components were retained or modified where appropriate. A redundant pair of Northrop AN/ASN-136 inertial navigation sets and a Lear Siegler AN/ASN-134 attitude heading reference set generated aircraft heading data. New angle-of-attack and air data sensors also were provided, as was a new AN/APN-224 radar altimeter and a modernized Norden Systems AN/APN-218 Doppler radar navigation set with OAS.

Beginning during 1985, all B-52Hs and some B-52Gs were equipped with the AN/APQ-166 "Strategic Radar" set, replacing the earlier OY-73/ASQ-176 radar set. This involved fitting new controls and displays, a new antenna electronics unit, an improved radar processor, and a modified radar antenna. The primary contractors were Boeing for the antenna and antenna electronics, and Norden Systems for the radar processor and display generator.

An A/A-42G-11 Automatic Flight Control System (AFCS) to assist the pilot was built into the MA-2 autopilot. This system provided both "steering" and "non-steering" modes of operation. In the steering mode (for low-level flying and air refueling) the aircraft still could be flown with the yoke and rudder. In the non-steering ("hard autopilot") mode, the aircraft was flown with the pitch and roll trim knobs. In either mode the OAS also could automatically command a reference heading to provide a stable bombing platform.

A new Sperry digital AFCS is being installed in all B-52G/H aircraft under a $116 million retrofit program. The goal of the new system is to achieve a significant increase in reliability. The digital unit has a new control panel that streamlines operations, and also deletes the servo switches on the pilot's left side panel. The new DAFCS is a two-axis system (pitch and roll) which provides steering and non-steering modes. A bomb mode allows the autopilot to be integrated with the OAS. The autopilot does not provide commands to the aircraft rudder, nor does it have any automatic approach interface capability.

Other avionics originally installed on the aircraft included: AN/AIC-10A (B-52G) or AN/AIC-18 (B-52H) interphone; two AN/ARC-34 UHF command radios; either an AN/ARC-58 or an AN/ARC-65 HF liaison radio; AN/ARN-21(either) or AN/ARN-118 (B-52H only) TACAN radio; AN/ARN-14 VHF omni range radio; AN/ARN-31 (either) or AN/ARN-67 (B-52H only) glide slope indicator; AN/ARN-32 marker beacon; AN/APN-150 radar altimeter; AN/APN-69 aerial rendezvous radar; and an AN/APX-64 IFF/SIF set.

Avionics upgrades to both the B-52G and B-52H have resulted in the aircraft carrying: either an AN/AIC-10A (B-52G) or AN/ARC-18 (B-52H) interphone; AN/ARC-164 UHF command radio; AN/ARC-190(V) HF liaison radio; AN/ASC-19 AFSATCOM system that includes an AN/ARC-171(V) auxiliary UHF command radio; AN/ARN-118 TACAN radio; AN/ARN-14 VHF omni range radio; AN/ARN-31 or AN/ARN-67 glide slope indicator; AN/ARN-32 marker beacon; AN/APN-224 radar altimeter; AN/APN-69 aerial rendezvous radar; and an AN/APX-64 IFF/SIF set.

Antennas for the radios are installed in various locations on the aircraft, with the No. 1 UHF blade antenna being on the bottom centerline of the fuselage just aft of the rear landing gear, and the No. 2 UHF blade antenna on the centerline of the upper forward fuselage between the defensive position ejection hatches. The IFF antenna is directly behind the No. 2 UHF antenna. The entire upper portion of the vertical stabilizer acts as the antenna for the HF liaison radio.

An AN/ASC-19 AFSATCOM system is installed including a terminal with a printer and keyboard, a satellite antenna, and a receiver/transmitter with a modem and encrypting equipment. The AFSATCOM terminal is a UHF radio system that provides both teletype satellite communications and line-of-sight UHF voice command capability. The UHF antenna is mounted in the normal No. 2 UHF antenna location, and the satellite antenna is mounted under a bulged fiberglass radome immediately aft of the UHF antenna.

ELECTRO-OPTICAL VIEWING SYSTEM (EVS)

Both the B-52G and B-52H were modified to incor-

All-white testbed **B-52G, 58-0182,** of the Air Force Flight Test Center, at Edwards AFB, during November of 1984. This aircraft supported various test program systems including miscellaneous items for the ALCM and the Rockwell B-1.

Camouflaged AGM-28B "Hound Dog", 61-2118, mounted on **B-52G 54-2582,** of the 456th BW, Beale AFB on alert at Hill AFB, Utah, on February 23, 1975. At the time, the AGM-28 was nearing the end of its operational career.

B-52H-150-BW, 60-0043, of the 19th BW, Homestead AFB, Florida on December 28, 1966. Aircraft is in early "bare metal" scheme with gloss white anti-glare paint on select panels. White dogleg on tail delineates HF antenna.

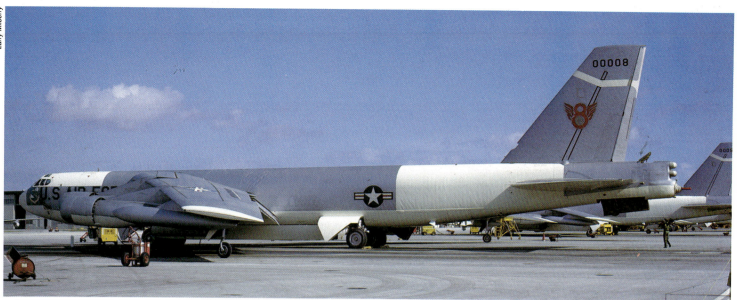
B-52H-135-BW, 60-0008, of the 19th BW, Homestead AFB. Red winged "8" indicates 8th Air Force. This particular aircraft participated in a Royal Air Force bomb competition on December 28, 1966. Nose art stated, "Dear Rocky not to win is a very bad thing."

B-52H-135-BW, 60-0003, of the 7th BW in "Strategic" scheme. Aircraft is in the middle of its gear retraction sequence. Low sun angle and associated reflection give impression of glossy paint on vertical fin tip.

B-52H-155-BW, 60-0046, of the 92nd BW, Fairchild AFB transient at Carswell AFB on November 1, 1988. AGM-28 pylon with multiple ejector racks is visible under left wing inboard of engine pylon.

porate the AN/ASQ-151 electro-optical viewing system (EVS), consisting of a Westinghouse AN/AVQ-22 steerable low-light level television (STV) unit, a Hughes AN/AAQ-6 forward looking infrared (FLIR) unit and an OD-86 data presentation group. The EVS provides crewmembers with a visual presentation of the area ahead of the aircraft for low-level penetration during both day and night missions. To accomplish this function, the EVS utilizes the steerable STV and FLIR to supply video, which is displayed on monitors at the pilot's, copilot's, navigator's and radar-navigator's positions. Since the EVS can be manually positioned to a wide range of angles generally forward of the aircraft's flight path, it also is used as an aid in air refueling rendezvous, formation flight and navigation position fixing. The EVS also receives input signals from the OAS, terrain avoidance radar and the attitude and heading systems, which are converted to symbology suitable for TV display and are overlayed on the EVS monitors.

The EVS sensors are located in independently steerable turrets on the underside of the aircraft just aft of the nose radome. The STV turret is on the left side of the aircraft, and the FLIR turret is on the right. Each turret rotates in azimuth to follow the position of its sensor during operation, but rotates to the aft (or stow) position when the sensor is not in use. The turrets are provided with optical windows to protect the sensors, and have wash facilities to remove debris from the windows during flight. The wash cycle is accomplished with the turret in the stowed position, is completed in 30 seconds and uses approximately 1.5 gal. of water (at 160°F and 500 psi). Roughly 14 gal. of demineralized water are stored in an electrically heated water tank located in the FLIR turret fairing and is enough for nine wash cycles.

The AN/AVQ-22 STV system is made up of the camera assembly, a camera electronics unit, and a control panel located at the radar-navigator's station. It provides a quality picture across a wide range of light conditions, day or night. Automatic light control circuits are used to adjust the picture as the ambient light situation changes during flight, though the crewmembers also have manual contrast and brightness controls independent of each other's monitors or system output. The STV can be adjusted to view scenes ±45° of aircraft centerline in azimuth and ±15° vertically from the camera mounting surface, which corresponds approximately to the aircraft waterline. A flash protector is built into the system that "stops down" the STV camera quite rapidly when bright flashes of light, including the sun and moon, are encountered.

The AN/AAQ-6 FLIR system consists of a scanner assembly, signal processor and a control panel, again located at the radar-navigator's station. The FLIR provides a real-time infrared display that can be adjusted in azimuth and elevation to the same limits as the STV. The FLIR scanner detects thermal (infrared) radiation that is processed by the signal processor and displayed on the EVS monitors.

Each crewmember (pilot, copilot, navigator and radar-navigator) can select either FLIR or STV independent of the other crewmembers. A steering priority system is installed to ensure the pilots can immediately select the direction of view they need during low level operations. Wide and narrow fields of view are available for use with both systems, with the narrow field of view equating to a telephoto-type picture. Viewing areas for the STV and FLIR are:

	Wide field-of-vision		Narrow field-of-vision	
	Vertical	Horizontal	Vertical	Horizontal
STV	16.8° ± 1.0°	22.4° ± 1.0°	5.6° ± 1.0°	7.5° ± 1.0°
FLIR	15.0° ± 0.6°	20.0° ± 0.6°	5.0° ± 0.2°	6.7° ± 0.2°

The EVS displays a video picture of the outside scene, either FLIR or STV as selected by the individual pilot. In the upper left corner is indicated airspeed. In the top center is time-to-go and the FCI (flight command indicator) which are generated by the OAS. FCI is essentially a heading command marker. On the right hand side in a vertical format is a radar altimeter display. On the left side is the elevation carrot and on the bottom center is the azimuth carrot. Each has symbology showing deflection from center. Fiducial marks are provided as an EVS aimpoint reference. A variety of other data and symbology can be presented on the EVS simultaneously with the FLIR or STV picture, including:

Terrain Trace and Horizontal Reference Line (HRL); Sensor Elevation; Sensor Azimuth; Clearance Plane Setting (CPS) [only with Strategic Radar]; Fiducial Marks; Pitch & Roll Bars.

There are four ways to position or control each sensor: VECTOR, CRAB. FIXED and control by the radar-navigator/navigator:

In VECTOR stabilization, the selected sensor is always slaved to the flight vector of the B-52. Azimuth and elevation information is derived from the AHRS, OAS, and Doppler radar. On aircraft not modified with Strategic Radar, elevation is obtained from an angle-of-attack vane on the fuselage side. When either pilot selects TA video on his EVS control panel, the selected sensor is automatically commanded to VECTOR.

In FIXED stabilization, the selected EVS sensor is slaved to the aircraft waterline.

In CRAB stabilization, the sensor is slaved to the cross-wind crab angle. However, the pilot who has control of the sensor may manually move the sensor throughout the ±45° in azimuth by using the knob provided on the pilots' EVS control panels.

The navigators can manually position the EVS sensors for a variety of requirements. The sensors may also be slaved to the OAS crosshairs or "target direct". The navigators can not select the three modes discussed above.

With the EVS installation, the round CRTs (TA scopes) for the ACR were deleted. Instead, terrain avoidance information is presented on the EVS in PROFILE mode. Terrain 45° either side of the aircraft's track is displayed with selectable range gates of 3, 6, and 10 miles. The terrain clearance plane may be set from 200 to 3,000 ft. without the strategic radar, or from 200 to 1,500 ft. with it.

EW SYSTEMS

The B-52 series has been modified many times to improve its ECM capabilities, the most recent being a continuation of the "Rivet Ace" program. The various ECM installations have, somewhat after the fact, been assigned "phase" numbers to identify a general equipment configuration. Currently, over 6,000 lbs. of ECM equipment is carried by each B-52G/H in active service. A quick overview of the first five "phases" is provided for reference purposes, with a more detailed look at the systems installed during Phase VI.

First-generation B-52s had nine jammer stations available for various ECM equipment. A need for additional power was recognized during the design of the B-52G, and that model was equipped with an additional five stations. The B-52H introduced two additional jammer stations, and three dedicated receiver stations, and the B-52Gs later were brought up to this standard. Several additional stations have been added to both aircraft over the years, and the aircraft have been equipped with a bewildering variety of ECM equipment.

Phase 0 (1956 - 1958): This was the initial operational configuration for the B-52, and was carried primarily by the B-52B and early B-52Cs. The equipment consisted of one AN/APR-9B radar intercept receiver, one AN/APR-14 radar intercept receiver, one AN/APS-54 radar warning receiver, fourteen AN/ALT-6B CW jamming transmitters, and two AN/ALE-1 chaff dispensers.

Phase I (1959-1961): Originally installed on late B-52Cs and B-52Ds and probably retrofitted to B-52Bs, this phase consisted of an AN/APR-9B radar intercept receiver, one AN/APR-14 radar intercept receiver, one AN/APS-54 radar warning receiver, ten AN/ALT-6B CW jamming transmitters, two AN/ALT-13(V) barrage-jamming systems, one AN/ALT-15H high-band jamming set, one AN/ALT-16 barrage-jamming system, and two AN/ALE-1 chaff dispensers.

Phase II/III (1961-1963): Typical of equipment carried by most operational B-52s during this time period, this "phase" consisted of an AN/APR-9B radar intercept receiver, one AN/APR-14 radar intercept receiver, one AN/APS-54 radar warning receiver, one AN/ALR-18 automated set-on receiving set, five AN/ALT-6B CW jamming transmitters, two AN/ALT-13(V) barrage-jamming systems, two AN/ALT-15H high-band jamming sets, one AN/ALT-15L low-band jamming set, one AN/ALT-16 barrage-jamming system, six AN/ALE-20 flare dispensers, and eight AN/ALE-24 chaff dispensers.

Phase IV (1964-1966): This phase drastically increased the amount of EW hardware aboard B-52s. The basic equipment consisted of one AN/ALR-20 countermeasures receiving set, one AN/APR-25 radar homing and warning (RHAW) system, one AN/ALR-18 automated set-on receiving set, five AN/ALT-6B or AN/ALT-22 CW jamming transmitters, two AN/ALT-13(V) barrage-jamming systems, two AN/ALT-15H high-band jamming sets, one AN/ALT-15L low-band jamming set, two AN/ALT-16 barrage-jamming system, six AN/ALE-20 flare dispensers, eight AN/ALE-24 chaff dispensers and two AN/ALE-25 forward firing chaff dispenser pods (B-52G/H only).

The AN/ALE-25 dispenser pod was designed to be carried on the small pylons located between the engine nacelles on each wing. This Boeing manufactured pod was approximately 13 ft. long, weighed 1,100 lbs. and required one electrical connection for installation. Each pod held 20 Tracor AN/ADR-8 2.5 in. folding fin chaff rockets which could be fired manually or automatically. The holes in the nose cone were filled with protective covers which loosened at the moment of launch. The system was installed on the last 18 production B-52Hs, and subsequently retrofitted to the rest of the B-52G/H fleet. The pod was retired from service in September 1970.

Phase V (1967-1969): Originally known as Rivet Rambler, this configuration was installed primarily on the B-52D model, although some of the equipment also found its way onto B-52Gs that served in SEA. As installed, it consisted of one AN/ALR-18 automated set-on receiving set, one AN/ALR-20 countermeasures receiving set, one AN/APR-25 RHAW system, four AN/ALT-6B or AN/ALT-22 CW jamming transmitters, two AN/ALT-16 barrage-jamming systems, six AN/ALT-28 or AN/ALT-13(V) barrage-jamming systems, two AN/ALT-32H high-band jamming sets, one AN/ALT-32L low-band jamming set, six AN/ALE-20 flare dispensers, and eight AN/ALE-24 chaff dispensers.

Some B-52Gs committed to Southeast Asia were modified to carry a Westinghouse AN/ALQ-119(V) ECM pod on the pylons originally installed for the AN/ALE-25 forward firing chaff pods. A single AN/ALQ-119(V) pod was carried under each wing. This modification was performed by Westinghouse and Boeing when the aircraft rotated back through the U.S. for maintenance.

Phase VI (1970-continuing): This phase originally was initiated under ECP-1551, also known as Rivet Ace, and is fitted exclusively to B-52Gs and B-52Hs. The updates initially were projected to cost $362.5 million, but the price tag is more likely to be in excess of $1.5 billion. Currently, many of the updates originally installed as part of Phase VI are being replaced by newer equipment, being called Phase VI+. A B-52G (58-0204) has served as the prototype for most of the Phase VI modifications. A 40 in. constant-chord extension to the fuselage aft of the horizontal stabilizer's trailing edge was added by Phase VI during 1970-1977 to house the additional equipment being installed. The antennas and radomes added during Phase VI created enough additional drag to decrease the range of the B-52G/H by 1.1%, independent of altitude. As a measure of the amount of work required, the initial Phase VI update required more than 9,000 man-hours of labor per aircraft.

AN/ALR-20A. This Electronic Resources Company developed, Tasker, Inc. produced countermeasures receiving set is capable of simultaneously surveying, detecting and displaying all radio frequency transmissions in the frequency band covered. The on-board bombing-navigation system and fire control system radio transmitters blank the receiving set to prevent display of their transmitted signals. Antennas are located in a small fairing just ahead of the windscreen on the extreme nose, on the left wingtip, and in the extreme aft fuselage, next to the tail turret.

AN/ALR-46(V). Dalmo Victor digital radar warning receiver that receives, analyzes and displays threat data to alert the EWO and gunner of possible threats. The system provides both an audio and video presentation which shows the type, azimuth and relative range of the threat. The AN/ALR-46 ties into the AN/ALQ-155 power management system, and receives blanking information from the OAS and FCS. The system is a significant modification of the older Itek AN/APR-25 RWR previously installed in the B-52.

AN/ALQ-117. Active countermeasures set manufactured by ITT Avionics. Improvements over earlier systems include adding frequency discrimination to existing PRF sorting, a programmable capability for responding to new threats, and a monopulse detection capability. Antennas are located in fairings on each side of the nose, just below the pilot's windscreen, and on the sides of the aft fuselage just above the trailing edge of the horizontal stabilizer. An additional antenna in the extreme aft fuselage above the tail turret (in the spot previously used by a TV camera) is used on the B-52G, while the B-52H has two additional antenna, one just above and one just below the 20mm gun turret. Two AN/ALQ-117 sets were installed in all B-52G/H aircraft, and were functionally replaced by the AN/ALQ-172.

AN/ALQ-122. Multiple false-target generator system manufactured by Motorola Government Electronics

B-52H-145-BW, 60-0022, of 7th BW at Carswell on May 5, 1985. '0022 was one of last three ASQ-38 equipped aircraft in 7th. Weathered paint is evident.

B-52H-145-BW 60-0026, of 319th BW at Grand Forks AFB, August 31, 1979. Standard paint and markings. 319th Bomb Wing insignia is on right side of fuselage.

B-52H-145-BW, 60-0028, taxis in at Carswell after a ferry flight with 12 external ALCMs. Pylons and missiles painted in "gunship" gray.

B-52H-145-BW, 60-0031, of 410th BW as it appeared at Salina, Kansas, airshow in May 1967. Bare metal with gloss white undersides and panels.

B-52H, 60-0034, "Slightly Dangerous" of 410th BW, taxis at Ellsworth AFB on September 1, 1989. Rainbow on tail is in shades of red and blue.

B-52H, 60-0040, of 7th BW shows "toned down" paint variation. White radome is still installed though forward fuselage has wrap-around gray.

B-52H-150-BW, 60-0041, of the 449th BW at McCoy AFB, Fla., for SAC Bomb/Nav meet in 1970 or 1971. ALE-25 underwing pylon is installed without rocket pod.

B-52H, 60-0046, from 5th BW at RAF Marham for 1981 RAF bombing meet. "Minot the Magician" is nose art, with "BEST in SAC" inscription below wing patch.

B-52H-155-BW 60-0048 of the 28th BW at Ellsworth AFB in October 1985. Paint pattern on rudder indicates it was scavenged from another aircraft.

B-52H, 60-0049, in landing configuration. Airbrakes position 4, the standard landing configuration, is evidenced by the 40 deg. spoiler deflection.

B-52H-B5-BW, 60-0004, of the 410th BW taxis at K.I. Sawyer AFB on September 8, 1986. Open auxiliary inlet doors are an obvious H-model indicator that the engines are running (on the ground). Three years later this aircraft was the last B-52H in SAC still in this paint scheme.

B-52H-145-BW, 60-0029, of the 7th BW at Carswell AFB on November 29, 1988. Noteworthy is sun-bleaching of paint and corrosion control touch-ups. Rub area on fuselage where stabilizer pivots is F.S. 36118 gray.

B-52H-165-BW, 61-015, of the 410th BW at K.I. Sawyer AFB on September 8, 1986. SIOP paint scheme with fully toned-down F.S. 36081 gray nose was standard prior to conversion to more recent gray-on-gray schemes.

B-52H-170-BW, 61-021 "Iron Eagle" of the 7th BW with full load of AGM-86B ALCMs (for munitions load training). Camouflage was single-tone F.S. 36081 gray overall. Nose art heralded this aircraft as the first CSRL B-52H.

B-52H-170-BW, 61-018, at Carswell AFB on November 26, 1984. SIOP scheme was complemented by full color 7th BW patch on forward section of fuselage just under cockpit windscreen. Aircraft visible to left in photo are on alert.

B-52G (left) and **B52H** (right) pilot/co-pilot forward instrument panels. EVS monitors dominate both crew positions. Major difference is B-52H's caution light panel consolidated just to the right of and below the pilot's flight instruments. Standard flight director system is "mirrored" at both stations and is common to both aircraft.

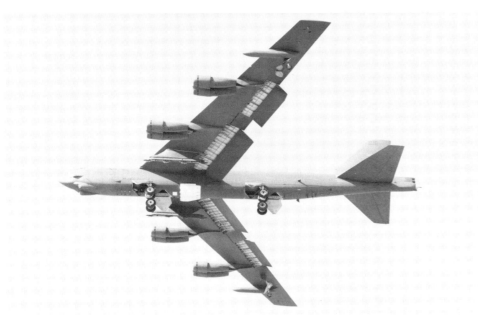

B-52H, 60-0051, of the 7th BW makes low approach with external AGM-28 pylons, MERs, and "Giant Fish" pod loaded. "Fish" pod occupies forward one-third of bomb bay. Bomb doors are disabled with pod fitted.

Group. AN/ALQ-122 automatically searches for, acquires and tracks signals, and generates a narrowband, low-duty-cycle ECM program to deny range and azimuth information to the tracking radar. These low-level signals are linearly amplified by AN/ALT-16A transmitters aboard the aircraft. Primary victim radars are ground controlled intercept, height finders, early warning and acquisition radars. Also known as "SNOE" (Smart Noise Operation Equipment).

AN/ALQ-153. Tail warning set produced by Westinghouse Electronic Warfare Division. This is a rear-looking, range-gated, pulse-Doppler radar that detects and discriminates approaching missiles and aircraft. The set provides target information, alerts the crew, and initiates chaff and/or flare countermeasures. Development tests were completed in 1976, and the first two operational units delivered in April 1980 for installation on a B-52H. Blisters on each side of the vertical stabilizer house antennas positioned to receive aft and outboard.

Several photographs of a B-52G with a large pod on the tip of the left horizontal stabilizer have been published with the pod identified as a tail warning radar. This was the losing RCA AN/ALQ-127 system that was in competition with the AN/ALQ-153 for the B-52 contract. Although no test reports have been made public, it is thought that the location of the antenna would have prevented full coverage to the right side of the aircraft.

AN/ALQ-155. Northrop designed power management system. This is a fully automatic countermeasures receiving and transmitting system capable of jamming or confusing enemy radars. The AN/ALQ-155 is capable of providing various power outputs covering a wide variety of frequencies. The transmitter units are liquid cooled, and ten units are installed in the B-52G/H. Two directional antennas are installed in the nose radome, eight flush omni antennas are installed on the bottom of the forward fuselage and two small conical omni antennas on the lower sides of the aft fuselage.

AN/ALQ-172. This is a significant update of the AN/ALQ-117 developed under the "Pave Mint" program by ITT Avionics. The AN/ALQ-172 will identify each specific threat individually and counter it with a specific ECM program optimized against that threat. If a threat can not be specifically identified, the system will respond with a "generic" program. The Pave Mint installation in the B-52G uses the core AN/ALQ-172(V)1 avionics but does not replace the early AN/ALQ-117 fixed-horn antennas. This configuration achieved operational status in September 1986. The full-up AN/ALQ-172(V)2 system currently installed on the B-52H replaces the fixed-horn antennas with electronically steerable phased-array antennas. This system reached operational status on the B-52H during mid-1988.

AN/ALT-16A. Hallicrafters (also Northrop/Raytheon/Litton) produced jammer used to linearly amplify a low-level signal generated by the AN/ALQ-122 system aboard the aircraft. The AN/ALT-16A is a high-power barrage-jamming system capable of denying the enemy range and number of aircraft information, and degrading azimuth information. A single AN/ALT-16A was fitted to early B-52Gs, although two jammers later were fitted to each B-52G and B-52H. Antennas are located in the extreme nose, and on the top and bottom of the aft fuselage just ahead of the leading edge of the vertical stabilizer.

AN/ALT-32H. Hallicrafters (also Motorola/Northrop/Raytheon) produced jamming transmitter set designed to jam enemy radar and communications. The "H" designates that this transmitter covers the "high" part of its assigned frequency band. Capable of noise-modulated spot or barrage-jamming. Two transmitter sets are installed on each aircraft, with each set consisting of a control indicator, power supply, transmitter and antenna. The system blade antennas are located on the lower left and right sides of the fuselage.

AN/ALT-32L. Basically similar to the AN/ALT-32H set, except covering the "low" portion of its assigned frequency band. The single system is installed with its antenna located on the right wing tip.

AN/ALE-20. Twelve of these Dynalectron designed flare ejectors are located in the aft fuselage of each B-52G/H. Each dispenser holds 16 AN/ALA-17 flares. The AN/ALE-20 flare ejector provides a means of selecting the number of flares to be fired and the time interval between the flares. The flares may be programmed to fire in bursts of one, two or three flares at intervals of between 2 and 20 seconds. The flares also may be salvoed at a rate of one flare every 65 milliseconds.

AN/ALE-24. Four Lundy AN/ALE-24 chaff dispensing systems are located in each wing of the B-52G/H in the area previously used by the aileron actuators and controls. The chutes for these dispensers appear as slots with rollers in them on the underside of the wing between the two flap sections. Locating the dispensers in the wings yields an effective countermeasures capability due to the high air turbulence, a large lateral separation between dispensers, and simultaneous ejection of chaff packages from both wings in bursts of two, four, or six packages. The wing location also reduces chaff contamination to the aircraft. The B-52G originally was equipped with AN/ALE-1 chaff dispensers in the same location, but was modified early in its career to carry the same AN/ALE-24 as installed on the B-52H from the beginning.

ARMAMENT:

DEFENSIVE SYSTEMS

The B-52G originally was equipped with an AN/ASG-15 fire control system and four M3 0.50 machine guns in a Bosch-Arma MD-9 hydraulically operated remote tail turret. Each gun is provided with 600 rounds of ammunition. The search antenna, which covers 120° in elevation and 166° in azimuth, is located in a large fairing in the extreme aft fuselage, above the tail turret. The track antenna is located in the center of the turret itself, between the guns, and covers 25° in both azimuth and elevation. Originally a TV camera was mounted between the turret and the search antenna radome to provide the gunner with a visual indication of what was happening. This camera was replaced by an AN/ALQ-117 antenna during the Phase VI ECM update.

A new AN/ASG-33 fire control system has been developed for the B-52G, although whether it will be deployed remains a question. The system has a single antenna that performs both the search and track functions located in the upper radome that originally housed the search radar. In search mode, the radar covers a conical scan area aft of the aircraft 90° in elevation and 135° in azimuth. The radar has an effective range of 20,000 yards. The AN/ASG-33 upgrade also installs electric gun chargers instead of the previous pneumatic ones and improves the ammunition feed system to increase its reliability. A new gun recorder, using VHS format video tape, is installed to record the fire control system's operations.

The B-52H is equipped with an Emerson modified AN/ASG-21 fire control system directing a single General Electric M61-A1 *Vulcan* cannon with 1200 rounds of ammunition in a GE-designed hydraulically operated gun laying mount in the tail. The system consists of two radar subsystems, either of which is capable of automatically searching for and tracking a target. The fire control system can track only one target at any one time thus allowing the other radar to remain in search, giving the system a modified search with a track capability.

B-52G/H PHASE VI DEFENSIVE AVIONICS SYSTEMS

ADM-20 (GAM-72) QUAIL

The GAM-72 Quail was developed by McDonnell Aircraft Corporation as a one-flight, minimum cost, minimum weight decoy missile for tactical use. The missile package as installed in the rear of the B-52 bomb bay consisted of a right and left launcher and four missiles, two per launcher. The missile was designed to carry an offensive system that enabled it to duplicate a B-52's radar signature and hence confuse and reduce the effectiveness of enemy radar-controlled air defense and infrared detection systems.

Preliminary design of the Quail was started by McDonnell in 1955 with the first powered flight occurring during November 1958. Many of the early air vehicles were equipped with parachute recovery systems to enable them to be reused. The AF test program for the YGAM-72 culminated on 24 June 1960 with the successful near-simultaneous launching of three Quails from a B-52G in an operational-type pattern, and the missile was declared operational shortly thereafter. On 18 November 1960 the first production GAM-72A was launched successfully.

The GAM-72 was 12 ft., 10.6 in. long, spans 5 ft., 4.5 in. when the wings were spread and weighed 1,230 lbs. loaded. It was 3 ft., 3.5 in. high when the wings were spread and the fins deployed, but was only 2 ft., 1.7 in. high when everything was folded up. The wing had 45.0° of sweep on its leading edge, and provided 28.01 sq. ft. of lifting area.

The missile was divided into four basic sections: forward body, aft body, lift and control surfaces, and engine. The forward body contained the flight control system components and some offensive systems and was constructed of fiberglass and honeycomb skin attached to laminated fiberglass longerons, although some aluminum was used in high stress areas. The aft body contained the engine air intake ducts, engine cooling ducts, fuel tanks, and additional offensive systems and was of conventional longeron and frame-type construction with aluminum alloy skin. The engine air intake and cooling ducts were made of fiberglass. The missile was powered by a single General Electric J85-GE-7 turbojet installed in the lower part of the aft body section of the missile.

The modified delta planform wings were mounted high on the sides of the missile aft body at a constant 1.5 degree negative incidence and zero dihedral. They were designed to fold downward along the sides of the aft body for stowage aboard the carrier aircraft. A folding vertical fin was mounted approximately midspan on each wing, and a fixed ventral fin was mounted on each wingtip. The upper vertical fin was folded outboard against the wing by mechanical linkage during wingfold. The wings were of conventional aluminum sheet metal construction, each containing two main spars, and auxiliary elevon spar, and a magnesium alloy tip casting. The upper fins were constructed of an aluminum alloy skin and rigid polyurethane foamed-in-place core sandwich and were attached to the upper wing surface by extruded continuous type hinges. The lower fins were constructed of polyester resin glass fiber molded laminate skin and rigid polyurethane foam core sandwich. The elevons were of conventional aluminum construction.

Two complete launch gear assemblies capable of supporting two missiles each were installed in the rear of the B-52 bomb bay. Launch control panels were located at the navigator's station. The primary function of the system was to support four missiles within the B-52 bomb bay and then to extend the missiles, one at a time, and launch them into free flight. If an extended missile could not be satisfactory launched, it could be jettisoned. If a left or right launch gear assembly failed or malfunctioned, the gear and any attached missiles could be jettisoned. In the event of a major emergency, the complete missile package could be jettisoned. Loading of the missiles into the bomb bay was accomplished utilizing the quick load configuration. In this configuration, a "package", consisting of four missiles and the complete launch gear assembly, was built up and mounted in the carrier aircraft as a unit.

In 1963 all 533 GAM-72A Quail decoys built under contract AF34(601)-14644 were modified for low-level flying and redesignated GAM-72B (ADM-20C). This relatively simple modification added a barometric switch for terrain avoidance and altered the missile's wiring system. A total of 585 GAM-72s were produced, and the missile was retired from service during 1978.

OFFENSIVE WEAPONS

During their Southeast Asia deployment in 1972-73, B-52Gs could carry conventional weapons only in the bomb bay. Subsequent conventional weapons modifications began in earnest with the conception of the Strategic Projection Force in 1980. Concurrent with the retirement of the B-52D fleet, the 69 non-ALCM capable B-52G's received a modification (TO 1B-52G-777) that installed wiring for external pylons and weapons as well as internal and external bomb release interval counters (BRIC). Beginning in 1985, a similar modification (TO 1B-52H-702) was installed in all B-52Hs, and the 777 mod subsequently was expanded to include ALCM-capable B-52Gs.

The B-52G/Hs are capable of carrying a variety of conventional weapons internally, using two basic bomb bay configurations. The first uses three cluster racks of nine stations each, for a total of 27 internal weapons. This configuration is used for 500-750 pound-class munitions. The second is two clip-in racks with four stations each for a total of eight internal weapons. This configuration is used for 2,000 pound-class weapons. The bomber also can carry a variety of free-fall nuclear bombs, such as the B28, B43, B53, B61 and B83.

The aircraft can also carry weapons on a single pylon suspended from each wing between the fuselage and inboard engine nacelle. The pylons originally were installed to carry the AGM-28 Hound Dog missile, which subsequently has been retired from service. There currently are three external configurations: AGM-28-pylons with two MERs per pylon for a total of 24 external weapons; stub-pylons with two MERs per pylon for a total of 24 external weapons; or stub-pylons with heavy stores adapter beams (HSAB) capable of carrying 6 Harpoons or 9 other weapons per wing. It should be noted that the stub-pylons are only compatible with non-ALCM B-52Gs.

Designation	Internal Cluster	Internal Clip-In	External MER	External HSAB	Weight (lbs.) Class/Actual
CBU-24B/B	27	—	—	18	750/830
CBU-49B/B	27	—	—	18	750/830
CBU-52B/B	27	—	24	18	750/785
CBU-58/B	27	—	24	18	750/820
CBU-71/B	27	—	24	28	750/820
M36 cluster	27	—	—	—	750/900
*Mk 82 GP	27	—	24	18	500/531
*Mk 82 Snakeye	27	—	24	18	500/560
*Mk 82 AIR	27	—	24	18	500/554
Mk 84 GP/AIR	—	8	—	10	2,000/1,970
M117GP	27	—	24	18	750/823
M117R	27	—	24	18	750/880
M117D	27	—	24	18	750/880
Mk 36 DST	27	—	24	18	500/560
MC-1	—	—	24	18	750/636
M129 leaflet	18	—	—	18	750/varies
MJU-1/B	27	—	—	18	750/varies
BDU-48 practice	9	—	8	—	none/10
Mk 40	—	—	—	18	1,000/1,060
Mk 55 mine	—	8	—	12	2,000/2,120
Mk 56 mine	—	8	—	12	2,000/2,055
Mk 60 mine	—	8	—	10	2,000/2,399
AGM-84 Harpoon	—	—	—	12	none/1,145

* Also applies to BDU-50 (concrete Mk 82 with same fins)

The "common strategic rotary launcher" (CSRL) was developed by Boeing for use in the B-52H, Rockwell B-1B and Northrop B-2. The CSRL is capable of carrying 8 ALCMs or 8 B83, 8 B61, or 4 B28 nuclear weapons. Development of the CSRL was initiated in 1982, and the first unit began flight testing during September 1985. A $44.5 million contract to initiate CSRL production was awarded to Boeing during February 1986 to cover five rotary launchers and their support equipment. A total of 104 CSRLs are expected to be purchased, with the 7th BW at Carswell AFB becoming the first wing to receive the CSRL during the last part of 1988. Each launcher costs approximately $1.8 million.

AGM-28 HOUND DOG

Part of the original B-52G capability called for the carriage of two North American GAM-77 (AGM-28) Hound Dog air-to-surface stand-off missiles. A single missile was transported under each wing, attached to the aircraft with special pylons that were equipped with the necessary support, launch and control systems mounted internally.

Hound Dog was 42.5 ft. long, 9.3 ft. high with a 12.17 ft. wingspan. The missile used a W28 nuclear warhead, and had a canard configuration, with a trapezoid wing and a swept vertical tail. Trailing edge flaps on the wing provided roll control and a conventional rudder provided directional control. The 2.3 ft. diameter fuselage was of reinforced semi-monocoque construction fabricated primarily of aluminum alloys. The fuselage was divided into five sections: a removable nose cone; a forward

B-52H, 60-0052, of 7th BW is one of two "Giant Fish" capable B-52Hs. Forward bomb door segment is removed to accomodate pod. Controls are at gunner's station.

B-52H, 60-0053, of 319th BW at Grand Forks AFB on August 31, 1979. Short blue "star spangled sash" on camouflaged B-52's was unique to the 319th BW.

B-52H, 60-0057, of 410th BW at RAF Marham. "Invasion" stripes and "C-5D" coding represent World War II marks. "Someplace Special" and rainbow on nose.

B-52H, 60-0059, second flagship of 9th BS at Carswell, taxis with AGM-86B ALCMs. Squadron patch is in gray and black below enlarged "9" in nose number.

B-52H-165-BW, 61-002, of 410th BW taxis at K.I. Sawyer AFB on September 8, 1986. Inlet bypass doors are open, taxi lights are on, and EVS turrets are open. Full-color 410th BW patch is on nose.

equipment compartment containing the ammonia coolant (among other things); a cylindrical center section containing the autonavigator and the warhead; a single integral fuel tank and an aft equipment compartment housing the hydraulic reservoir and the electrical generator. The aerodynamic surfaces were of multi-spar construction with honeycomb sandwich skins. The engine nacelle contained a diffuser shell, which supported and enclosed the diffuser centerbody and translating spike; the cowl, which enclosed the engine; and the exhaust nozzle fairing.

Power was furnished by a single 7,500 lb. thrust Pratt & Whitney J52-P-3 engine which enabled a top speed of 2.1 Mach and a maximum range at high altitude of 700 miles. The missile's engine could be ignited while attached to the pylon, effectively giving the B-52 two additional engines. It was possible to refuel the missile from the B-52's fuel supply. On the GAM-77, a self-contained N-5G inertial guidance system was updated immediately prior to launch from a KS-120 astrotracker housed in the pylon. The astrotracker was moved into the missile itself on the GAM-77A.

During early October 1957, the AF officially designated North American's WS-131B missile the XGAM-77. A letter contract, AF33(600)-36040, had been dated 16 September and was a cost-plus-fixed-fee type, with the fee amounting to 6.5 percent. Boeing actually was listed as the prime contractor under contract AF33(600)-36208, and had responsibility for the total weapons system which comprised the *Hound Dog* in place on a modified B-52. Boeing also was responsible for the initial drop tests and for the design of the pylon, although they subcontracted the latter item to North American. The development of *Hound Dog* was not particularly easy, although it was fairly quick. In an effort to speed up the fielding of the weapon, production missiles were ordered, and accepted, before the first prototype had flown. By mid-February 1960, $610.8 million had been spent on its development and production, and this did not include government furnished equipment which added another $200 million to the total. Boeing's total for the modification to the B-52 fleet, including the bombing-navigation system, was $34,930,182.

The first inert drop test occurred on April 3, 1959, and the first powered flight of a XGAM-77 missile took place on April 23, 1959, achieving 1.7 Mach at 36,000 feet, which was somewhat less than expected. The first full inertial-guided flight of a production *Hound Dog* occurred on August 23, 1959 and the weapon officially entered service with SAC as WS-131B on December 21, 1959. On March 2, 1960 a B-52G, manned by a SAC crew from Eglin AFB, launched both *Hound Dog* missiles over the Atlantic Missile Test Range during a single flight. Then on April 12, another *Hound Dog* armed B-52G took off from Eglin, flew to the North Pole, then back to the east coast of Florida to score another successful launch. This 22 hr. flight covered 10,800 miles, and demonstrated that the *Hound Dog* could withstand prolonged captive-carry periods prior to being launched. During March 1960 the missile successfully demonstrated low-level launches and low-level attacks.

An updated version, the GAM-77A (AGM-28B) improved the accuracy of the missile, as well as taking care of some minor deficiencies in the original design. The design also included a slightly larger fuel tank, although the overall size of the missile did not change. This improved missile entered the inventory during 1961 and made up the significant part of the 703 unit *Hound Dog* production, although accuracy would continue to be marginal and the subject of intense debate. The GAM-77A was declared operational on February 1, 1961, and peak *Hound Dog* strength was attained in 1963 when SAC had 600 in the inventory. By January 1976 this had been reduced to 300, and the missile was retired from service by the end of 1976.

GAM-87A *SKYBOLT*

This still-born weapon had its origins with the WS-110A and WS-125A weapons systems that, for a while, were scheduled to replace the B-52 in AF service. Both of these had General Operational Requirements (GOR) which included an advanced air-to-surface missile. The *Skybolt* subsequently went through five separate sets of requirements, three demonstration programs, two program reevaluations and no less than thirty-seven separate proposals for its manufacture.

The situation in Britain was equally as confusing. The Royal AF was developing the *Blue Streak* intermediate range ballistic missile, but the Royal Navy was pushing to get it cancelled and to purchase Polaris submarine based missiles instead. When the U.S. decided to pursue the development of the GAM-87A during February 1960, the RAF, sensing that the *Blue Streak* battle already was lost, started pushing for the purchase of Skybolt. By June 1960 it was announced that Britain would not participate in the development effort, but would purchase 100 production *Skybolts*.

This agreement was unpopular in both countries, but for different reasons. The U.S. objected that the USAF was picking up all development costs, and that England would pay only for the production costs of the missiles it accepted. The British were angered by the fact that they were going to buy a critical piece of their independent nuclear force from another government. The projected cost of 1,000 missiles for the U.S. and 100 for Britain was $2.5 billion in FY60 dollars.

As it finally evolved, the weapon was an Air-Launched Intercontinental Ballistic Missile (ALBM) built by the Douglas Aircraft Company. Douglas won the contract to develop the missile under WS-138A on May 26, 1959 and shortly thereafter awarded contracts to Aerojet General to develop the propulsion system, to General Electric to develop the reentry vehicle and to Nortronics for the guidance system. Boeing and Avro assisted to ensure system compatibility with the B-52H and *Vulcan*. The original schedule called for an initial operational date of 1964.

The British carrier aircraft was to be an Avro *Vulcan* B.2 carrying a *Skybolt* under each wing. All *Vulcans* built after June 1960 had internal wing strengthening and pick-up points for the *Skybolt*. The first of several inert drop tests from a *Vulcan* B.2 was carried out on December 9 1961 over the West Freugh range to the north of Scotland.

Each B-52 was to carry four missiles on unique two-missile launchers suspended from the weapons pylon under each wing. Starting during 1961 many captive-carry and inert drop tests were conducted from B-52Gs and B-52Hs. The first five live-fire tests conducted during 1962 were considered failures, although the sixth was listed as an unqualified success. Part of the problem was that the missile had to know exactly where it was in three-dimensional space at the exact moment of firing, this when the carrier aircraft was moving at 600 mph. The technology of the 1960s simply did not allow that sort of accuracy, although there were potential solutions to the problem in sight. However, the missile was cancelled by President Kennedy during December 1962, bowing more to political and economic pressures than technical ones, although the missile was significantly behind its development schedule.

President Kennedy apparently considered transferring the entire Skybolt program to the British to continue, but the cost was deemed too great for the British defense budgets of the era. In an effort to appease the British, the U.S. offered to sell Polaris submarine launched ballistic missiles (SLBM) on favorable terms. The British accepted reluctantly, but later came to realize the decision was a good one.

AGM-69A SHORT-RANGE ATTACK MISSILE

The Boeing AGM-69A SRAM is powered by a Thiokol SR-75-LP-1 restartable solid-fuel two-pulse rocket motor and is equipped with a General Precision/Kearfott inertial guidance system. Unidynamics manufactured the missile's safe/arm/fuze subsystem, while Litton Industries

B-52H-165-BW, 61-010, with full load of four GAM-87 "Skybolt" air launched ballistic missiles. This early aircraft is virtually devoid of protruding ECM antennas. Markings and colors are standard.

supplied the inertial reference units. Stewart-Warner designed and built the terrain clearance sensor and Delco Electronics supplied the computer. The SRAM is 14 ft. long, 17.5 in. in diameter and weighs 2,230 lbs. Range varies from 30 to 100 miles and top speed is approximately 2.5 Mach. A W69 nuclear warhead is used. Total additional weight of the SRAM equipment, less missiles, is 10,296 lbs.—2,208 lbs. for the avionics and related equipment, 3,722 for the rotary launcher, and 4,366 for the external pylons, which no longer are used.

The first live flight was made on July 29, 1969, and the first all-SAC launch was accomplished on September 24, 1970. The missile became operational on August 4, 1972 with the 42nd BW at Loring AFB. Production was halted on July 30, 1975 after 1,521 missiles had been delivered. Each B-52 can carry up to 8 SRAMs internally on a rotary launcher that is preloaded prior to installation in the B-52. External SRAM pylons, each capable of carrying six SRAMs on standard MAU-12 ejector racks, were deployed to a number of wings during the 1970s, but were withdrawn from service by the early 1980s.

AGM-86B AIR LAUNCHED CRUISE MISSILE

The AGM-86B Air Launched Cruise Missile (ALCM) is an air breathing stand-off weapon produced by Boeing Aerospace. It actually started out life as the Subsonic Cruise Armed Decoy (SCAD), a replacement for the *Quail* first proposed during 1966. The idea was even if the Soviets figured out how to differentiate between the decoy and the B-52, if the decoy was nuclear-armed and seeking a target, the Soviets still would have to expend resources to shoot it down. Additionally, the new missile was to address *Quail's* two most serious shortcomings: limited range and large physical size. Two versions of the missile were proposed, a SCAD-A for the B-52 and a longer range SCAD-B for the B-1. The next five years would be spent on debating the relative merits of an "armed" decoy missile, with the result being cancellation of the project during June 1973.

The SCAD led directly to the ALCM-A (AGM-86A), followed by the extended range vehicle (ERV), and finally by the even larger ALCM-B (AGM-86B), which was the only variant produced. The route by which it got there was confusing, and largely politically motivated. The AF started out by pointing out that SCAD's chances for penetration were the same as the B-52's since it radiated the same radar image via electronics. This led to the question of its chances with the electronics turned off. It turned out that the chances were significantly better, and the long political battle over the future of manned penetrating bombers was revived, just as it had been in the 1950s. On June 28, 1973 the Department of Defense directed that $22 million from funds previously committed to SCAD should go into cruise missile technology studies to be coordinated with the Navy's sea-launched cruise missile program (the two ended up using similar guidance systems). The next six years would be spent selecting contractors for the ALCM and continuing to debate the role of the manned bomber. Two contractors eventually competed for the ALCM contract, Boeing with their AGM-86B, and General Dynamics with the AGM-109H Tomahawk derived from the Navy's submarine launched cruise missile. A competitive fly-off was staged during 1979, and Boeing subsequently was awarded a $141,570,990 contract on May 2, 1980 for the production of 225 missiles. The first B-52G equipped with the AGM-86B was delivered to the 416th BW, which became operational with the weapon during December 1982. The last of the 1,815 missile production run was delivered during October 1986.

The missile is stored with its wings, elevons and vertical tail folded, deployment taking less than two sec. after the weapon is dropped from the carrier aircraft. In its flight configuration, the missile is 20 ft. 9 in. long, spans 12 ft., has a body diameter of 24.5 in. and weighs 3,200 lbs. Power is provided by a single Williams International F107-WR-100 turbofan engine rated at 600 lbs. static thrust. Top speed is approximately 500 mph and range is about 1,500 miles. A single W80 nuclear warhead is carried in the fuselage forward of the wing, this warhead being a development of the W69 device used on the SRAM. The weapon free-falls for a short time immediately after release, with the wings being fully deployed two seconds after launch and the engine up to full thrust three seconds later. By the time ALCM is flying under its own power, it has fallen about 450 ft.

Guidance is accomplished by an inertial navigation set which is updated every 60 sec. from the B-52's INS prior to launch. Once launched and at low level, a "terrain contour matching" (TERCOM) system using data from an

B-52H, 61-010, of 449th BW at Barksdale AFB for bomb comp on November 16, 1974. Wing patch is just visible forward of wing. Yellow winged "2" for 2nd Air Force and pre-EVS nose are noteworthy.

B-52H, 61-012, of 7th BW on climbout at Carswell AFB. ALQ-155 antenna array just aft of the open EVS turret windows are evident. Left look angle of turrets indicates wind drift compensation.

B-52H, 61-013, of 28th BW at Ellsworth in October 1985 with toned down radome but without gray wrap-around camouflage on nose. Vertical tail was evidently neglected during most recent paint job.

B-52H, 61-018, of 410th BW visiting Carswell AFB on February 3, 1987 after a weather divert from K.I. Sawyer AFB. Rainbow is gray and black. Low-visibility blue and gray wing patch is on nose.

B-52H, 61-021, "Iron Eagle" of 7th BW, at Carswell on January 11, 1989. Aircraft is in single color (F.S. 36081) version of Strategic camouflage paint. Nose art depicts "1021" as first CSRL equipped B-52H.

on-board radar altimeter takes over. This system compares data from the radar altimeter with stored map information to fly a preprogrammed route. The stored map contains information gathered primarily from satellite data regarding terrain features such as hills, rivers, vegetation, etcetera. TERCOM itself is not a new concept, and it bears at least a superficial resemblance to the ATRAN (automatic terrain recognition and navigation) system used in the TM-61B Matador and TM-76A/B Mace ground-launched cruise-missiles of the mid-1950s (Mace B was not retired until after 1970).

B-52G/H's with cruise missile integration (CMI) can carry 12 ALCMs externally, six on each wing pylon. Further, CSRL-modified B-52Hs can carry an additional 8 ALCMs on the internally-loaded CSRL.

AGM-84 HARPOON

The AGM-84 *Harpoon* missile is an all-weather, sea-skimming, anti-ship missile armed with a 488.5 lb. conventional warhead. It is built by McDonnell Douglas Astronautics and first was fielded by the U.S. Navy during 1977. It can be launched from a variety of aircraft, ships and submarines. Over 4,000 missiles have been delivered to the Navy, the AF and eighteen foreign countries.

The B-52/*Harpoon* weapon systems consists of a "Surface Attack Guided Missile, Air" (either an AGM-84A-1, AGM-84C-1 or AGM-84D-1) and associated Launch Control Equipment (LCE). The B-52 aircraft has the capability of carrying 12 *Harpoon* missiles on two Heavy Stores Adapter Beams (HSAB), one under each wing, with six missiles per HSAB. The *Harpoon* can be fired singularly or in salvo, one from each wing. The LCE requires that the aft station missiles be launched prior to the forward station. This ensures that jet exhaust from the forward station missiles does not damage the weapons on the aft station.

The missile is 12 ft. 7 in. long, 13.5 in. in diameter and has a wing span of 36 in. When fueled with JP-5 the missile weighs 1,145 lbs. The Teledyne CAE J402-CA-400 turbojet engine provides 660 lbs. of thrust for approximately eight min. The missile flies in a cruciform configuration (i.e.; with the wing in an "X" configuration rather than a "+" configuration) at high subsonic speeds with over-the-horizon ranges. The missile is capable of being launched from low or high altitudes, with engine start either before or after launch depending on the B-52 altitude and airspeed. No data link from the launching platform is required by the missile after launch.

The early model AGM-84A-1 has a terminal "pop-up" maneuver just prior to target impact. The AGM-84C-1 flies at sea skimming altitudes all the way to the target without the "pop-up" maneuver. The AGM-84D-1 uses the same flight profile as the AGM-84C-1, but has an extended range due to its use of JP-10 fuel instead of JP-5. A new version of the AGM-84, called "SLAM" (standoff land attack missile) might also be fitted to the B-52G in the future. This new missile is about 25 in. longer and 200 lbs. heavier than the anti-ship version and entered flight test during late 1988.

AGM-129A ADVANCED CRUISE MISSILE

On March 2, 1989, A B-52H based at Edwards AFB conducted the first captive-carry test of the Convair AGM-129A Advanced Cruise Missile (ACM) over the Cold Lake Test Range in Alberta, Canada. The AGM-129A is similar in size to the AGM-86B ALCM it is scheduled to supplement, not replace. The missile has a slightly triangular-shaped fuselage that tapers into a pointed nose. An engine air inlet protrudes from the underside of the missile's rear fuselage. There are folding fins at the missile's tail, stowed flush with the sides of the fuselage. The ACM's "stealth" design and advanced propulsion and guidance systems will offer improved range and accuracy over the existing ALCM. Propulsion is provided by a Williams International F112 turbofan engine, and range is thought to be at least 10% greater than ALCM's. It is expected that a W80 nuclear warhead will be carried. The highly classified ACM program is more than a year behind schedule, and Congress has been reluctant to release further funding for the program until the AF successfully demonstrates six free-flight tests. McDonnell Douglas recently has been selected as an eventual second source producer of the missile. The B-52H's of the 644th BMS at K.I. Sawyer AFB have been modified for ACM integration, but the missile itself is not yet operational.

AGM-136A TACIT RAINBOW

Northrop's AGM-136A Tacit Rainbow anti-radiation (ARM) missile is designed to seek out and destroy enemy air defense radar systems. Unlike most ARMs, Tacit Rainbow is designed to loiter on its own for extended periods and automatically attack enemy radars when they are activated. As of the fall of 1989, five of a planned 25 test flights had been performed, three from a B-52G and two from a Navy A-6E. The first test, on 30 March, resulted in the crash of the missile about 30 minutes after launch. The other two B-52G tests, conducted on May 17, and May 31, were termed "very successful". The missiles were launched from a rotary launcher mounted in the B-52G's bomb bay. Each B-52 can carry up to 30 Tacit Rainbows on three rotary launchers. The missile is powered by a Williams WR36-1 turbofan engine, is 8 ft. 4 in. long, has a 61.5 inch wingspan and carries a 40 lb. high-explosive warhead. The AF plans a small buy of 90 missiles in FY90 to continue testing, but must certify to Congress before October 31, 1989 that the test program is proceeding satisfactorily. Total cost of the program, for 12,000 AF and Navy variants, is estimated at $3.72 billion. A number of problems were experienced early in the program, mainly because of a lack of quality control at Northrop, and a decision on low-rate initial production is not expected to be made before mid-1990.

POWERPLANTS:

B-52G

The B-52G is powered by eight Pratt & Whitney model J57-P-43WB (JT3C) engines. Although the engine was designed, and many built by P&W (hence the letter "P" in the designation), a second source for the engine was the Ford Motor Company, and these engines are designated J57-F-43WB. Each engine has a maximum standard day sea level uninstalled thrust rating of 13,759 lbs. with water injection and 11,200 lbs. without water injection. The engines are "flat rated" which enables them to produce a constant wet rated thrust across a wide range of temperature and pressure altitude conditions. The engines are mounted in pairs, in four nacelles suspended below the wings. They are numbered in the conventional manner from left to right 1 to 8, and the nacelles are similarly numbered, with nacelle number one containing engines 1 and 2, and so forth. Each nacelles contains two engines, a firewall, a nose cowl, and right and left lower and upper side cowl panels. The nose cowl is a single unit attached to the strut and encloses both engine air inlets. The upper side cowl panel covers the top half of the engine from the nose cowl to the aft end of the tail pipe. The lower side cowl panels covers the lower half of the engine from the nose cowl to the aft end of the tailpipe. The lower and upper cowl panels are provided with support rods to secure the panels in the wide-open ("butterfly") position.

The engines are identical with exception of the engine-mounted accessories. A starter is installed on the lower side of each engine between the engine-mounted accessories. An engine driven hydraulic pump is installed on the lower right side of engines 1, 3, 4, 5, 6, and 7, and a 70/90 KVA generator is installed on the lower left side of engines 1, 3, 5, and 7. A dual capacity engine-driven water pump is installed on the lower left side of engines 2, 4, 6, and 8.

The design of the J57 started during 1947, was finalized in 1949, and production began during February 1953. It is a continuous flow, non-afterburning, gas turbine engine consisting of two multistage axial-flow compressors, eight combustion chambers and a split, three-stage turbine assembly. The basic engine is 38.88 in. in diameter, 167.53 in. long and weighs approximately 4,234 lbs.

The axial-flow dual compressor has a nine-stage low pressure (N1) unit and a seven-stage high pressure (N2) unit. The rotors and discs in both units are constructed of heat-resistant steel. The N2 unit has a pressure ratio of 13:1 with a mass air flow of 200 lbs. per sec. The compressors supply air to the annular combustion chambers where fuel is added and burned. The gas stream from the combustion section enters the turbine section giving energy to the split, three-stage turbines, that drive the dual compressors. The first turbine stage drives the N2 compressor by a hollow shaft. The second and third stages drive the N1 compressor by a concentric shaft through the hollow N2 compressor shaft. A gearbox at the bottom of the engine provides external drive pads for the starter, tachometer, fuel pump, and Hamilton-Standard fuel control units, and includes engine oil pressure transducers and oil scavenger pumps. The N1 rotor has three tachometer drive pads at the bottom of the air inlet case. An accessory drive adapter is attached to the lower aft part of the diffuser case, below the combustion section. The accessory drive provides power to operate the oil pump and various accessories (water pump, hydraulic pump, CSD).

The engine has two automatically activated overboard bleed valves between the N1 and N2 compressors to facilitate starting, improve acceleration, and to prevent surging by ducting low pressure air overboard during low power operation. HP compressor bleed air is used for various aircraft systems. An outer annular steel casing encloses eight Inconel alloy interconnected burner cans, each with six fuel nozzles. The fuel is ignited by two spark plugs located in burner cans No. 4 and 5, and the flame is propagated to the other burner cans by connecting flame tubes. The continuous combustion supplies heat for expanding the compressor air, increasing the velocity of the gas flow to the turbine. The turbine gases are discharged through a fixed area exhaust nozzle.

A water injection system is provided which allows water to be sprayed into both the engine compressor air inlet and the diffuser section of each engine for increased thrust during takeoff. The primary effect of the water injection is to cool the air, increasing the density and the mass airflow through the engine. The increased airflow, coupled with an automatic increase in fuel flow, provides added thrust. Water injection is accomplished by four dual-capacity engine-driven pumps installed on the lower left side of engines 2, 4, 6, and 8. Each pump provides the engine in that nacelle with a rated flow of 40,000 pounds of water per hour at a pressure of 385 to 440 psi. The 1,200 gallon water supply tank is located in the forward fuselage just aft of the crew compartment. The engine tailpipes are fitted with three internal lobes which serve as sonic vibration suppressors to reduce the damaging effect on the wing trailing edge structure caused by wet operation of the aircraft engines.

Eight throttles are mounted on the pilots' aisle stand to control the firewall fuel shutoff valves, throttle valves and water injection. Once the throttles are advanced from the closed position, essential dc power opens the firewall fuel shutoff valves provided the fire shutoff switches are pushed in. Simultaneously, if the corresponding engine starter switch is placed in the start position, essential dc power is applied to the engine ignition circuit. Other systems also are wired into the throttles. Advancing engines Nos. 3 and 5 or No. 4 and 6 to approximately 88% rpm (74 ° throttle throw) completes the flaps up warning horn circuit, sounding the warning horn if the aircraft is on the ground and flaps are not 100% down. When the throttles are advanced to open, or full throttle, with the water injection switch on, power is supplied to initiate water injection. Anytime a throttle is retarded to within about one inch of the IDLE indent, with any landing gear is not down and locked, a landing gear warning horn is sounded.

The throttles, when viewed from the side, look like a "Y" or wishbone. The upper knobs are bent outboard slightly for spacing and each has a different height for ease of individual throttle adjustment. The lower set of knobs are closely spaced and all at the same height so that the pilot can operate all eight engines together for ease of overall power application. A mechanical detent at the idle position is provided to prevent closing any throttle without first lifting up on the upper knobs. A throttle brake lever is located just to the right of the throttles. It is used to change the amount of force necessary to adjust the throttles. Its most common uses are to lock the throttles at takeoff power setting once committed for takeoff, and to aid in maintaining cruise power setting, particularly when "throttle creep" is experienced.

B-52H

The B-52H is powered by eight Pratt & Whitney model TF33-P-3 (JT3D-2) low-bypass turbofan engines. The engines are mounted in pairs, in four nacelles suspended below the wings, and are numbered in the same manner as the B-52G. The first and second stage N1 compressor rotor blades are longer than the remaining ones, comprising the fan portion of the engine. The cowlings on the B-52H are noticeably different from the B-52G/J57 cowling combination. The forward, or wrap cowl, has a larger diameter than the afterbody cowl. The wrap cowl covers the fan and compressor stages of the engine as well as the fan bypass ducts. Fan bypass air is discharged axially out the bypass ducts over the surface of the afterbody cowling. Also on the forward cowl area are eight auxiliary air inlet doors (sometimes called suck-in doors), provided to assist in allowing ample airflow across the compressor inlet. These doors are springloaded to the closed posi-

B-52H-170-BW, 61-025, of 28th BW at Ellsworth, October 1985. Lower section of #8 engine wrap cowl is removed for maintenance.

B-52H, 61-031, during "Quick Start" test at Boeing Wichita. Simultaneous cartridge start of all eight engines produces large, noxious smoke cloud.

B-52H-175-BW, 61-038, of 7th BW approaches Carswell runway 17. Extreme nose low attitude on approach offers pilot excellent view of landing environment.

B-52H, 60-0054 of 7th BW onloads fuel from 68th AREFW KC-10A, 86-0031. "Flex" of wings in flight is typical. "Fort Worth Texas" tail logo is noteworthy.

tion and are opened by differential pressure felt by each door. The factors impacting on this differential pressure include Mach number, engine thrust setting and aircraft angle-of-attack. The doors are open during ground operation and usually close after take-off as the aircraft accelerates to flap retraction speed. At higher speeds they are virtually always fully closed. During traffic pattern operations, they vary in position, sometimes fluttering, and often will close when engines are retarded to idle in the pattern (such as for simulated engine out approach work).

The TF33 is basically a J57 with the first three stages of the J57 compressor removed and two fan stages added. Of considerably larger diameter than the compressor, the fan extends well outside the compressor casing and is contained in a short-chord annular shroud. The third-stage turbine on the J57 was enlarged and a fourth stage added to provide the power necessary to drive the low-pressure compressor rotor and integral fan. A new short discharge duct was designed to exhaust the fan air well forward on the engine nacelle just after it passes through the fan. The TF33 produces 50% more take-off thrust (17,000 pounds) and 20% more cruise thrust than the J57, while giving a 13% improvement in specific fuel consumption.

The engines are identical with exception of the engine-mounted accessories, which are driven by way of an accessory gearbox using a shaft directly geared to the main shaft from the fist stage turbine to the low pressure compressor. A Sundstrand 120 KVA generator with a constant speed drive is installed on the lower left side of engines 1, 3, 5, and 7. Engine fan air is used for cooling the generators through an air-oil cooler and is vented from under the afterbody cowling. An engine-driven variable delivery hydraulic pump is installed on the lower right side of engines 1, 3, 4, 5, 6, and 7. An electrically controlled air-drive starter is installed on the lower side of each engines. All engines have a cartridge start capability.

An engine stall prevention system is provided to control the engine compressor surge bleed valves for prevention of stalls which are caused by crosswinds during ground operations. Because of unique inlet distortion combined with the TF33-P-3 engine compressor characteristics, stalls can occur in crosswinds of 10 knots or more with the winds more than 45° from the aircraft's heading, usually below 50 KIAS.

The B-52H throttles are the same as those on the B-52G. The flaps up warning horn sounds at about 75% rpm (45°). The major difference between the B-52G and B-52H throttles is the thrust gate on the B-52H. This adjustable mechanical gate was added after it was discovered that rapid, large throttle movements could cause a severe and uncontrollable pitch up. This gate is used to limit the amount of power applied by the pilots. At temperatures up to 100°F, the TF33 engines will produce takeoff rated thrust (TRT) with considerably less than full throttle; thus the thrust gate is provided to avoid overboosting engines or setting excessive or potentially hazardous power. Detents are spaced 5° apart on the outside of the throttle quadrant guide rail, numbered from 40 to 100°. A spring loaded scissor-type lever is used to set the gate. The thrust gate normally is adjusted to where it can be overpowered (i.e.; pushed through the gate) by about twice the force necessary to normally move all eight throttles together.

COMMON

All engine instruments are grouped together on the center instrument panel between the pilot and copilot. An engine pressure ratio (EPR) gauge, RPM gauge, exhaust gas temperature (EGT) gauge, and a fuel flow indicator is provided for each engine in a vertical format with individual engines read in sequence from left to right, 1 to 8. The oil pressure gauges are located in a small eyebrow panel just above the windscreen. Additionally, a total fuel flow gauge is located below the bank of main engine instruments to assist the pilots in power management.

The RPM gauges, or tachometers, are powered by engine driven tachometer generators and are fully independent of the B-52 electrical system. The tach generators measure the speed of the high-pressure compressor rotor. The EGT gauges also are independent of the aircraft electrical system,, and are powered by engine thermocouples. The EPR gauges run off 118 volt ac power and measure the differential between inlet and exhaust pressure. EPR is the only method for setting power in the B-52G/H.

On both the B-52G and B-52H, an engine fuel control

B-52H, 60-0020, from AFFTC and 31st TS in flight with 12 General Dynamics AGM-129 "Advanced Cruise Missiles" in only to-date unclassified photo of "ACM."

B-52 NUCLEAR PROFILE CHANGES

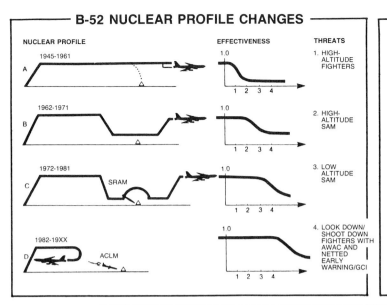

B-52G/H PRODUCTION

MODEL	SERIAL NUMBER TO	SERIAL NUMBER	# OF A/C	BOEING C/N TO	BOEING C/N
Contract Number AF33(600)-35992					
B-52G-75BW	57-6468 —	57-6475	8	W173 —	W180
B-52G-80-BW	57-6476 —	57-6485	10	W181 —	W190
B-52G-85-BW	57-6486 —	57-6499	14	W191 —	W204
B-52G-90-BW	57-6500 —	57-6520	21	W205 —	W225
Contract Number AF33(600)-34670					
B-52G-95-BW	58-0158 —	58-0187	30	W226 —	W255
B-52G-100-BW	58-0188 —	58-0211	24	W256 —	W279
B-52G-105-BW	58-0212 —	58-0232	21	W280 —	W300
B-52G-110-BW	58-0233 —	58-0246	14	W301 —	W314
B-52G-115-BW	58-0247 —	58-0258	12	W315 —	W326
Contract Number AF33(600)-37481					
B-52G-120-BW	59-2564 —	59-2575	12	W327 —	W338
B-52G-125-BW	59-2576 —	59-2587	12	W339 —	W350
B-52G-130-BW	59-2588 —	59-2602	15	W351 —	W365
Contract Number AF33(600)-38778					
B-52H-135-BW	60-0001 —	60-0013	13	W356 —	W378
B-52H-140-BW	60-0014 —	60-0021	8	W379 —	W386
B-52H-145-BW	60-0022 —	60-0033	12	W387 —	W398
B-52H-150-BW	60-0034 —	60-0045	12	W399 —	W410
B-52H-155-BW	60-0046 —	60-0057	12	W411 —	W422
B-52H-160-BW	60-0058 —	60-0062	5	W423 —	W427
Contract Number AF33(600)-41961					
B-52H-165-BW	61-0001 —	61-0013	13	W428 —	W440
B-52H-170-BW	61-0014 —	61-0026	13	W441 —	W453
B-52H-175-BW	61-0027 —	61-0040	14	W454 —	W467

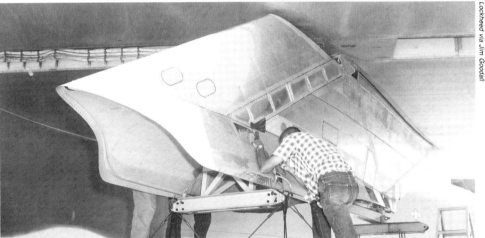

Lockheed D-21B Pylon is fitted to B-52H wing root assembly. Pylon was being statically tested for load-bearing ability, even though an extensive experience base had been generated with such pylons as a result of the X-15 program.

AGM-69A PRODUCTION

MODEL	SERIAL NUMBER TO	SERIAL NUMBER	# OF A/C
AGM-69A	71-0907 —	71-1028	122
AGM-69A	72-0601 —	72-1065	465
AGM-69A	73-0227 —	73-0706	480
AGM-69A	74-0189 —	74-0642	454
Total SRAM Production:			1,521
AGM-69A (cancelled)	74-1761 —	74-2060	300

GAM-72 (ADM-20) PRODUCTION

MODEL	SERIAL NUMBER TO	SERIAL NUMBER	# OF A/C
XGAM-72-1-MC	57-5752 —	57-5775	24
GAM-72-5-MC	59-2232 —	59-2243	12
GAM-72-10-MC	59-2244 —	59-2255	12
GAM-72A-15-MC	60-616 —	60-645	30
GAM-72A-20-MC	60-646 —	60-705	60
GAM-72A-25-MC	60-706 —	60-851	146
GAM-72A-30-MC	61-333 —	61-444	112
GAM-72A-35-MC	61-445 —	61-539	95
GAM-72A-40-MC	61-540 —	61-633	94
Total *Quail* Production:			585

[Note: GAM-72A later converted to AGM-20C]

GAM-77 (AGM-28) PRODUCTION

MODEL	SERIAL NUMBER TO	SERIAL NUMBER	# OF A/C
XGAM-77	59-2791 —	59-2867	77
GAM-77	60-2078 —	60-2247	170
GAM-77	60-5574 —	60-5603	30
XGAM-77A	60-6691 —	60-6699	9
GAM-77A	61-2118 —	61-2357	240
GAM-77A	62-0030 —	62-0206	177
Total *Hound Dog* Production:			703

AGM-86B PRODUCTION

MODEL	SERIAL NUMBER TO	SERIAL NUMBER	# OF A/C
AGM-86B	79-0244 —	79-0261	18 [1]
AGM-86B	80-0838 —	80-1062	225
AGM-86B	81-0078 —	81-0557	480
AGM-86B	82-0194 —	82-0633	440
AGM-86B	83-0143 —	83-0472	330
AGM-86B	84-0214 —	84-0453	340
Total ALCM Production:			1,815

Note 1: Pre-production missiles

GAM-87 PRODUCTION

MODEL	SERIAL NUMBER TO	SERIAL NUMBER	# OF A/C
XGAM-87A	61-2448 —	61-2449	2
GAM-87A	63-7310 —	63-7367	58
GAM-87A	63-9065 —	63-9071	7
Total *Skybolt* Production:			67

system on each engine automatically provides optimum engine performance at any throttle setting. This system makes it unnecessary to make any throttle adjustments to compensate for variations in inlet temperature, altitude or airspeed. Fuel from the fuel tanks is routed through the fuel supply system to fuel control units which meter fuel to each engine. The throttle provides basic engine power control and operates in conjunction with the fuel control units' pressure, speed and temperature sensing servos to position a throttle.

As originally built, only engines 4 and 5 contained cartridge-pneumatic starters, but operation "Quick Start", approved in 1974, modified all B-52Gs and B-52Hs to have cartridge-pneumatic starters on all eight engines to facilitate quicker reaction times and less dependence on ground support equipment. Prior to Quick Start, the other six engines relied on pneumatic only starters, using either an auxiliary air cart or air from an operating engine. Eight spare cartridges can be carried on the aircraft if needed. The starter turbine may utilize either low pressure air obtained from a ground source or from an operating engine through the air bleed system, or may utilize high-pressure gas generated from the burning solid propellant cartridge. Starter operation is basically the same for pneumatic or cartridge operation with the major difference being the temperature and pressure of the two gases.

Each engine is provided with an integral oil system which includes an oil tank with a minimum usable capacity of 6.8 gal. (7.1 gal. in B-52H) and a total capacity of 8.75 gal. (10.23 gal. in B-52H). From the tank, oil is supplied to gear-type engine-driven oil pressure pumps which supply the engine bearing and accessory drives. Scavenge pumps remove the oil from the engine compartment, route it through an oil cooler, and return it to the tank for reuse. No manual controls are provided for the oil system. B-52G aircraft have an airscoop-type oil-cooler, while B-52Hs use a fuel-oil cooler.

An air refueling system makes it possible to refuel the aircraft in flight from a boom-type tanker aircraft. An air refueling slipway and receptacle, which is covered by hydraulically operated slipway doors when not in use, is located on top of the fuselage slightly aft of the pilot's stations. When the air refueling boom nozzle is seated in the air refueling receptacle, it is held there by hydraulically operated latching toggles. A single point refueling system is fitted with the receptacle located forward of the left forward wheel well.

There are a total of 12 fuel tanks on the B-52G and B-52H. Of these, four are designated as main tanks, meaning they are the primary source of fuel for the engines, and the rest are designated as auxiliary tanks. Total fuel capacity is approximately 48,030 gal. The fuel supply system is designed so that the engines receive fuel from the nearest of four main tanks. The main tanks are integral wing tanks ("wet wing"); each tank has four boost pumps and normally supplies two engines. The No. 1 main tank supplies engines Nos. 1 and 2, the No. 2 main tank supplies engines Nos. 3 and 4, and so forth. The auxiliary tanks include two outboard wing tanks which are also integral wing tanks, an integral center wing tank, three fuselage tanks, and two nonjettisonable external tanks. The three fuselage tanks are not self-sealing. A crossfeed manifold system is provided that makes it possible to supply any engine from any tank. The fuel tanks have capacities as listed below:

Tank Name or location	Number of tanks	Usable Fuel (gallons)	Usable Fuel (pounds)
No. 1 and 4 Main	2	4,899	31,843
No. 2 and 3 Main	2	6,809	44,259
Mid Body	1	7,140	46,410
Forward Body	1	2,049	13,319
Aft Body	1	8,491	55,192
Outboard Wing	2	1,153	7,495
Center Wing	1	3,228	20,982
External	2	700	4,550

IN DETAIL:

B-52G GENERAL ARRANGEMENT DIAGRAM
TYPICAL

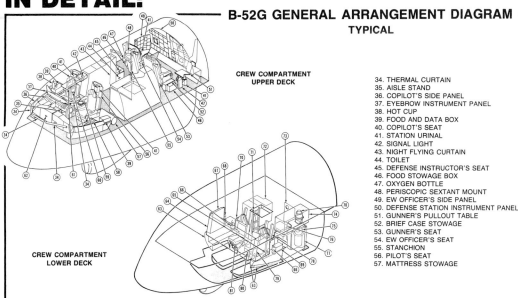

CREW COMPARTMENT UPPER DECK
CREW COMPARTMENT LOWER DECK

34. THERMAL CURTAIN
35. AISLE STAND
36. COPILOT'S SIDE PANEL
37. EYEBROW INSTRUMENT PANEL
38. HOT CUP
39. FOOD AND DATA BOX
40. COPILOT'S SEAT
41. STATION URINAL
42. SIGNAL LIGHT
43. NIGHT FLYING CURTAIN
44. TOILET
45. DEFENSE INSTRUCTOR'S SEAT
46. FOOD STOWAGE BOX
47. OXYGEN BOTTLE
48. PERISCOPIC SEXTANT MOUNT
49. EW OFFICER'S SIDE PANEL
50. DEFENSE STATION INSTRUMENT PANEL
51. GUNNER'S PULLOUT TABLE
52. BRIEF CASE STOWAGE
53. GUNNER'S SEAT
54. EW OFFICER'S SEAT
55. STANCHION
56. PILOT'S SEAT
57. MATTRESS STOWAGE

58. PILOT'S SIDE PANEL
59. INSTRUCTOR PILOT'S SEAT
60. PERISCOPIC SEXTANT CARRYING CASE
61. PILOT'S OVERHEAD PANEL
62. PILOT'S OVERHEAD PANEL
63. MISCELLANEOUS EQUIPMENT SHELF
64. NAVIGATOR'S INSTRUMENT PANEL
65. STATION URINAL
66. OXYGEN BOTTLE
67. NAVIGATOR'S SIDE PANEL
68. HOT CUP
69. FOOD STOWAGE BOX
70. DRINKING WATER CONTAINER
71. LADDER
72. REMOTE MODULES RACK
73. PRESSURE BULKHEAD DOOR
74. ELECTRONIC EQUIPMENT RACK
75. CENTRAL URINAL
76. INSTRUCTOR NAVIGATOR'S TAKEOFF-LANDING SEAT
77. POWER SUPPLY RACK
78. RADAR NAVIGATOR'S SEAT
79. RADAR NAVIGATOR'S SIDE PANEL
80. INSTRUCTOR NAVIGATOR'S DUTY SEAT
81. NAVIGATOR'S SEAT

B-52H GENERAL ARRANGEMENT DIAGRAM
TYPICAL

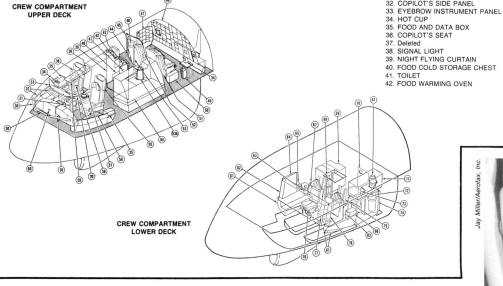

CREW COMPARTMENT UPPER DECK
CREW COMPARTMENT LOWER DECK

30. THERMAL CURTAIN
31. AISLE STAND
32. COPILOT'S SIDE PANEL
33. EYEBROW INSTRUMENT PANEL
34. HOT CUP
35. FOOD AND DATA BOX
36. COPILOT'S SEAT
37. Deleted
38. SIGNAL LIGHT
39. NIGHT FLYING CURTAIN
40. FOOD COLD STORAGE CHEST
41. TOILET
42. FOOD WARMING OVEN

43. DEFENSE INSTRUCTOR'S SEAT
44. FOOD STOWAGE BOX
45. OXYGEN BOTTLE
46. PERISCOPIC SEXTANT MOUNT
47. EW OFFICER'S SIDE PANEL
48. DEFENSE STATION INSTRUMENT PANEL
49. Deleted
50. BRIEF CASE STOWAGE
51. GUNNER'S SEAT
52. EW OFFICER'S SEAT
53. STANCHION
53A. DRINKING WATER CONTAINER
54. CREW BUNK
55. PILOT'S SEAT
56. PILOT'S SIDE PANEL
57. INSTRUCTOR PILOT'S SEAT
58. PERISCOPIC SEXTANT CARRYING CASE
59. PILOT'S OVERHEAD PANEL
60. PILOT'S INSTRUMENT PANEL

Pilots' instrument panel in B-52G, 58-0200. EVS monitors are prominent at both stations. Lower portion of copilot's front panel is the fuel panel with pump switches and quantity gauges.

B-52H pilots' overhead panel. Oxygen regulator and interphone panel are for instructor pilot.

Jay Miller/Aerofax, Inc.

39

B-52H pilot's left side panel. Hydraulic system panel is farthest forward panel on side bulkhead. Other panels include IFF, nuclear consent and pylon jettison switches, oxygen, interphone, lights.

B-52G throttle quadrant and aisle stand. Airbrake lever is left of throttles, drag chute handle right.

B-52H copilot's side panel. Generator control panel, oil temp gauge, and three-position starter switches are on side bulkhead. Other panels include HF radio, battery, CG/FLAS, and AHRS control.

B-52G pilot's side panel. Major difference between G and H side panel is water injection panel. Four selsyn indicators show pump pressure, eight lights indicate water pressure at engines.

B-52G copilot's side panel. Two position starters (start/off) are provided. B-52G has no oil temperature monitor system. Fuel system checkout panel is visible in upper right.

B-52H aisle stand and throttle quadrant. Central caution panel in background identifies B-52H.

B-52G PILOT'S STATION
TYPICAL

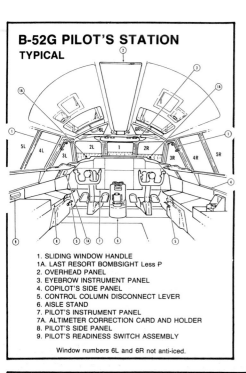

1. SLIDING WINDOW HANDLE
1A. LAST RESORT BOMBSIGHT Less P
2. OVERHEAD PANEL
3. EYEBROW INSTRUMENT PANEL
4. COPILOT'S SIDE PANEL
5. CONTROL COLUMN DISCONNECT LEVER
6. AISLE STAND
7. PILOT'S INSTRUMENT PANEL
7A. ALTIMETER CORRECTION CARD AND HOLDER
8. PILOT'S SIDE PANEL
9. PILOT'S READINESS SWITCH ASSEMBLY

Window numbers 6L and 6R not anti-iced.

B-52H PILOT'S STATION
TYPICAL

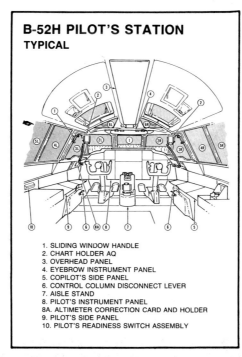

1. SLIDING WINDOW HANDLE
2. CHART HOLDER AQ
3. OVERHEAD PANEL
4. EYEBROW INSTRUMENT PANEL
5. COPILOT'S SIDE PANEL
6. CONTROL COLUMN DISCONNECT LEVER
7. AISLE STAND
8. PILOT'S INSTRUMENT PANEL
8A. ALTIMETER CORRECTION CARD AND HOLDER
9. PILOT'S SIDE PANEL
10. PILOT'S READINESS SWITCH ASSEMBLY

B-52H THERMAL CURTAINS

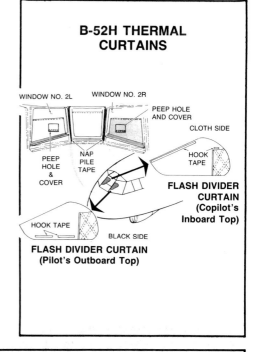

B-52G PILOT'S INSTRUMENT PANEL
Less L

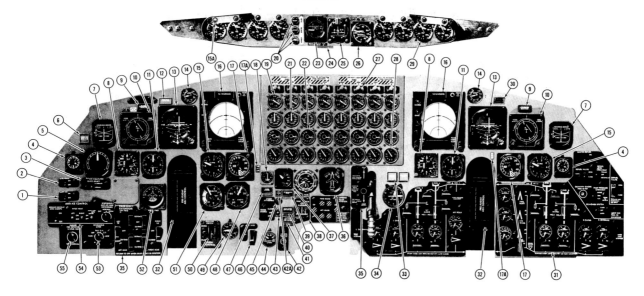

1. MACH INDICATOR SWITCH
2. BYRO POWER SWITCH
3. FLIGHT DIRECTOR COMPUTER GYRO SELECT SWITCH
4. CLOCK
5. LATERAL ERROR METER
6. TIME-TO-GO LIGHT
7. FLIGHT COMMAND INDICATOR
8. ALTIMETER
9. MARKER BEACON LIGHT
10. HORIZONTAL SITUATION INDICATOR
11. AIRSPEED INDICATOR
12. AUTOPILOT-DISENGAGED LIGHT
13. ATTITUDE-DIRECTOR INDICATOR
14. CLEARANCE PLANE INDICATOR
15. VERTICAL VELOCITY INDICATOR
15A. LOW OIL PRESSURE WARNING LIGHTS
16. TERRAIN DISPLAY INDICATOR
17. RADAR ALTIMETER
17A. RADAR ALTIMETER CAUTION LIGHT
18. LATERAL TRIM INDICATOR
19. ENGINE PRESSURE RATIO GAGES
20. AIR REFUELING LIGHTS
21. TACHOMETERS
22. EXHAUST GAS TEMPERATURE GAGES
23. ACCELEROMETER
24. MAGNETIC STANDBY COMPASS CORRECTION CARD
25. MAGNETIC STANDBY COMPASS
26. CABIN ALTIMETER
27. ENGINE FIRE SHUTOFF SWITCHES
28. FUEL FLOWMETERS
29. OIL PRESSURE GAGES
30. MASTER CAUTION LIGHT
31. FUEL SYSTEM PANEL (FIGURE 1-19)
32. TERRAIN PREFLIGHT ADJUST CONTROL
33. TIP PROTECTION GEAR WARNING LIGHT
34. TOTAL FUEL FLOW INDICATOR
35. LANDING GEAR CONTROLS (FIGURE 1-40)
36. CROSSWIND CRAB POSITION INDICATOR
37. WING FLAP POSITION INDICATOR
38. SAS CONTROL PANEL (FIGURE 4-27A)
39. BOMB DOORS OPEN LIGHT
40. BOMB DOORS NOT LATCHED LIGHT
41. HATCHES WARNING LIGHT
42. OXYGEN QUANTITY GAGE PRESS-TO-TEST SWITCH
42A. IFF MODE 4 LIGHT
43. BOMB DOOR SWITCH
44. TOTAL OXYGEN QUANTITY INDICATOR
45. STORE JETTISONED LIGHT
46. ANTISKID SWITCH
47. BOMB RELEASED LIGHT
48. TRUE AIRSPEED INDICATOR
49. OUTSIDE AIR TEMPERATURE GAGE
50. AUTOPILOT TURN CONTROL SELECTOR SWITCH
51. MACH INDICATOR
52. HEADING INDICATOR
53. WINDSHIELD WIPER SWITCH
54. ANTI-ICE CONTROL PANEL (FIGURE 4-7)
55. ENGINE FIRE DETECTOR SYSTEM TEST SWITCH

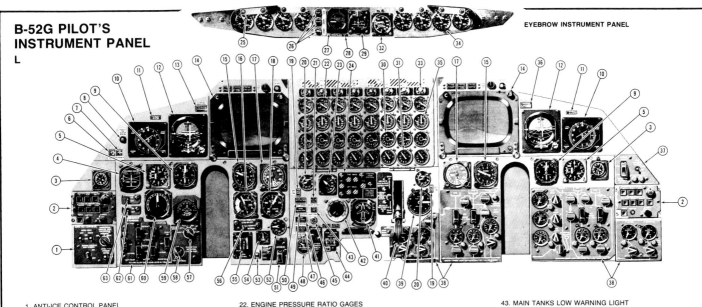

B-52G PILOT'S INSTRUMENT PANEL
L

1. ANTI-ICE CONTROL PANEL
2. EVS CONTROL PANEL
3. CLOCK
4. FLIGHT COMMAND INDICATOR
5. ALTIMETER
6. TIME-TO-GO LIGHT
7. IFF MODE 4 LIGHT
8. MARKER BEACON LIGHT TEST SWITCH
9. INDICATED AIRSPEED INDICATOR
10. HORIZONTAL SITUATION INDICATOR
11. MARKER BEACON LIGHT
12. ATTITUDE-DIRECTOR INDICATOR
13. AUTOPILOT DISENGAGED LIGHT
14. EVS MONITOR
15. VERTICAL VELOCITY INDICATOR
16. MACH INDICATOR
17. RADAR ALTIMETER
18. TRUE AIRSPEED INDICATOR
19. RADAR ALTIMETER CAUTION LIGHT
20. CLEARANCE PLANE INDICATOR
21. TIP PROTECTION GEAR WARNING LIGHT
22. ENGINE PRESSURE RATIO GAGES
23. WING FLAP POSITION INDICATOR
24. LANDING GEAR POSITON INDICATORS PANEL
25. LOW OIL PRESSURE WARNING LIGHTS
26. AIR REFUELING LIGHTS
27. ACCELEROMETER
28. MAGNETIC STANDBY COMPASS CORRECTION CARD
29. MAGNETIC STANDBY COMPASS
30. EXHAUST GAS TEMPERATURE GAGE
31. FUEL FLOWMETERS
32. CABIN ALTIMETER
33. ENGINE FIRE SHUTOFF SWITCHES
34. OIL PRESSURE GAGES
35. TACHOMETERS
36. MASTER CAUTION LIGHT
37. FUEL SCAVENGE SYSTEM PANEL
38. FUEL SYSTEM MANAGEMENT PANELS
39. TOTAL FUEL FLOW INDICATOR
40. LANDING GEAR LEVER
41. CROSSWIND CRAB POSITION INDICATOR
42. TOTAL FUEL QUANTITY INDICATOR
43. MAIN TANKS LOW WARNING LIGHT
44. SAS CONTROL PANEL
45. STORES JETTISONED LIGHT
46. BOMB RELEASED LIGHT
47. HATCHES WARNING LIGHT
48. TOTAL OXYGEN QUANTITY GAGE
49. BOMB DOORS OPEN LIGHT
50. BOMB DOORS NOT LATCHED LIGHT
51. ANTISKID SWITCH
52. OUTSIDE AIR TEMPERATURE GAGE
53. BOMB DOORS SWITCH
54. LATERAL TRIM INDICATOR
55. AUTOPILOT TURN CONTROL SELECTOR SWITCH
56. FLIGHT DIRECTOR COMPUTER GYRO SELECTOR SWITCH
57. WINDSHIELD WIPER SWITCH
58. ENGINE FIRE DETECTOR SYSTEM TEST SWITCH
59. HEADING INDICATOR (GYRO)
60. LATERAL ERROR METER
61. LANDING GEAR CONTROLS PANEL
62. MACH INDICATOR SWITCH
63. GYRO POWER SWITCH

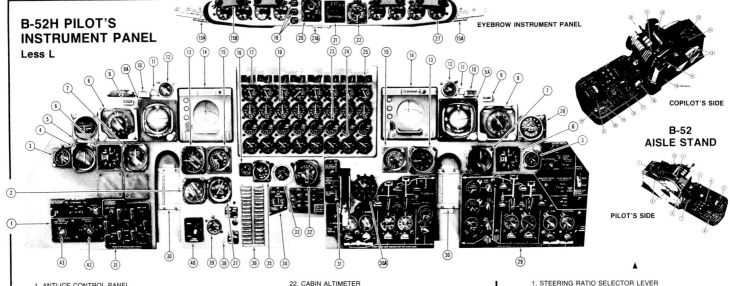

B-52H PILOT'S INSTRUMENT PANEL
Less L

1. ANTI-ICE CONTROL PANEL
2. MACH INDICATOR
3. CLOCK
4. LATERAL ERROR METER (AGM-28)
5. FLIGHT COMMAND INDICATOR
6. ALTIMETER
7. INDICATED AIRSPEED INDICATOR
8. HORIZONTAL SITUATION INDICATOR
9. MARKER BEACON LIGHT
9A. ATTITUDE-DIRECTOR INDICATOR
10. MASTER CAUTION LIGHT
11. FRL INDICATOR LIGHT
12. CLEARANCE PLANE INDICATOR
13. VERTICA VELOCITY INDICATOR
14. TERRAIN DISPLAY INDICATOR
15. RADAR ALTIMETER
15A. J-4 STANDBY HEADING SYSTEM CORRECTION CARD
15B. LOW OIL PRESSURE WARNING LIGHTS
16. LATERAL TRIM INDICATOR
17. ENGINE PRESSURE RATIO GAGES
18. AIR REFUELING LIGHTS
19. TACHOMETERS
20. ACCELEROMETER
21. MAGNETIC STANDBY COMPASS
21A. MAGNETIC STANDBY COMPASS CORRECTION CARD
22. CABIN ALTIMETER
23. EXHAUST GAS TEMPERATURE GAGES
24. FUEL FLOWMETERS
25. ENGINE FIRE SHUTOFF SWITCHES
26. (DELETED)
27. OIL PRESSURE GAGES
28. HEADING INDICATOR (GYRO)
29. FUEL SYSTEM PANEL
30. TERRAIN PREFLIGHT ADJUST CONTROL
30A. TOTAL FUEL FLOW INDICATOR
31. LANDING GEAR CONTROLS
32. CROSSWIND CRAB POSITION INDICATOR
33. TOTAL FUEL QUANTITY INDICATOR
34. SAS CONTROL PANEL
35. WING FLAP POSITION INDICATOR
36. CENTRAL CAUTION PANEL
37. TRUE AIRSPEED INDICATOR
38. BOMB DOOR SWITCH
39. OUTSIDE AIR TEMPERATURE GAGE
40. AUTOPILOT TURN CONTROL SELECTOR SWITCH
41. (DELETED)
42. WINDSHIELD WIPER SWITCH
43. ENGINE FIRE DETECTOR SYSTEM TEST SWITCH

B-52 AISLE STAND

1. STEERING RATIO SELECTOR LEVER
1A. THRUST GATE
2. AIRBRAKE LEVER
3. AUTOPILOT TURN AND PITCH CONTROLLER
4. AUTOPILOT SWITCH PANEL
5. CROSSWIND CRAB CONTROL KNOW
6. LANDING LIGHTS PANEL
7. LATERAL TRIM CUTOUT SWITCH
8. STABILIZER TRIM CUTOUT SWITCH
9. STABILIZER TRIM WHEEL AND INDICATOR
10. THROTTLES
11. THROTTLE BRAKE LEVER
12. PARKING BRAKE LEVER
13. AIR CONDITIONING PANEL
14. DRAG CHUTE LEVER
15. WARNING HORN SHUTOFF BUTTON (BEHINE)
16. WING FLAP LEVER
17. NAVIGATION SYSTEM SELECT PANEL
18. TERRAIN DISPLAY CONTROL PANEL
19. EMERGENCY ALARM MONITOR LIGHT
20. EMERGENCY ALARM SWITCH
21. RUDDER TRIM KNOB AND INDICATOR
22. CROSSWIND CRAB CONTROL CENTERING BUTTON

B-52H PILOT'S INSTRUMENT PANEL
L

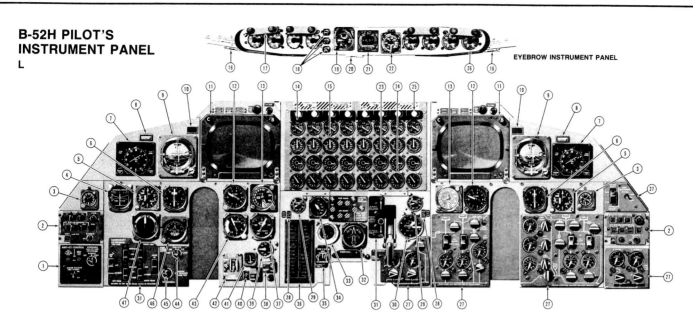

EYEBROW INSTRUMENT PANEL

1. ANTI-ICE CONTROL PANEL
2. EVS CONTROL PANEL
3. CLOCK
4. FLIGHT COMMAND INDICATOR
5. ALTIMETER
6. INDICATED AIRSPEED INDICATOR
7. HORIZONTAL SITUATION INDICATOR
8. MARKER BEACON LIGHT
9. ATTITUDE-DIRECTOR INDICATOR
10. MASTER CAUTION LIGHT
11. EVS MONITOR
12. VERTICAL VELOCITY INDICATOR
13. RADAR ALTIMETER
14. ENGINE PRESSURE RATIO GAGES
15. TACHOMETERS
16. J-4 STANDBY HEADING SYSTEM CORRECTION CARD
17. LOW OIL PRESSURE WARNING LIGHTS
18. AIR REFUELING LIGHTS
19. ACCELEROMETER
20. MAGNETIC STANDBY COMPASS CORRECTION CARD
21. MAGNETIC STANDBY COMPASS
22. CABIN ALTIMETER
23. EXHAUST GAS TEMPERATURE GAGES
24. FUEL FLOWMETERS
25. ENGINE FIRE SHUTOFF SWITCHES
26. OIL PRESSURE GAGES
27. FUEL SYSTEM PANELS
28. RADAR ALTIMETER CAUTION LIGHT
29. CLEARANCE PLANE INDICATOR
30. TOTAL FUEL FLOW INDICATOR
31. LANDING GEAR CONTROLS
32. CROSSWIND CRAB POSITION INDICATOR
33. TOTAL FUEL QUANTITY INDICATOR
34. WING FLAP POSITION INDICATOR
35. SAS CONTROL PANEL
36. CENTRAL CAUTION PANEL
37. TURE AIRSPEED INDICATOR
38. CENTRAL CAUTION RESET PANEL
39. OUTSIDE AIR TEMPERATURE GAGE
40. BOMB DOOR SWITCH
41. LATERAL TRIM INDICATOR
42. AUTO PILOT TURN CONTROL SELECTOR SWITCH
43. MACHMETER
44. WINDSHIELD WIPER SWITCH
45. ENGINE FIRE DETECTOR SYSTEM TEST SWITCH
46. HEADING INDICATOR (GYRO)
47. LATERAL ERROR METER (AGM-28)

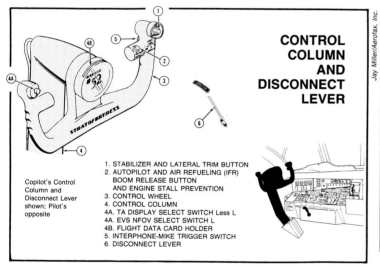

CONTROL COLUMN AND DISCONNECT LEVER

Copilot's Control Column and Disconnect Lever shown; Pilot's opposite

1. STABILIZER AND LATERAL TRIM BUTTON
2. AUTOPILOT AND AIR REFUELING (IFR) BOOM RELEASE BUTTON AND ENGINE STALL PREVENTION
3. CONTROL WHEEL
4. CONTROL COLUMN
4A. TA DISPLAY SELECT SWITCH Less L
4A. EVS NFOV SELECT SWITCH L
4B. FLIGHT DATA CARD HOLDER
5. INTERPHONE-MIKE TRIGGER SWITCH
6. DISCONNECT LEVER

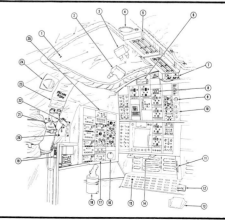

B-52H overhead and "eyebrow" panels. UHF radio control heads, air refueling panels, oil pressure gauges, accelerometer, and standby compass are visible.

B-52G EW OFFICER'S STATION Less R
TYPICAL

1. ESCAPE HATCH
2. SIDE PANEL FLOOD LIGHT
3. CONSOLE FOOD LIGHT
4. UPPER AISLE AND ENTRY LIGHT
5. ECM CIRCUIT BREAKER PANEL
6. UPPER AIR OUTLET
7. ASM LOCK-UNLOCK SWITCH PANEL
8. CLOCK
9. EMERGENCY ALARM LIGHT
10. TEMPERATURE CONTROL PANEL
11. REFUEL VALVE EMERGENCY CONTROL HANDLE
12. SPECIAL WEAPONS MANUAL LOCK HANDLE STOWAGE BRACKET
13. SPECIAL WEAPONS MANUAL LOCK HANDLE
14. CLIPBOARD STOWAGE BOX
15. INTERPHONE FOOTSWITCH
16. ASH TRAY
17. INTERPHONE CONTROL PANELS
18. RELIEF CONTAINER
19. OXYGEN BOTTLE RECHARGER
20. LIGHTING CONTROL PANEL
21. PORTABLE OXYGEN BOTTLE
22. SPOT LIGHT
23. ESCAPE ROPE CONTAINER
24. ECM DOME LIGHT
25. OXYGEN REGULATOR

B-52H EW OFFICER'S STATION Less R
TYPICAL

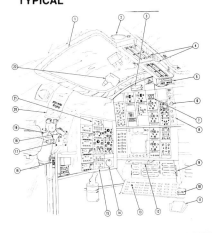

1. ESCAPE HATCH
2. UPPER AISLE AND ENTRY LIGHT
3. UPPER AIR OUTLET
4. ECM CIRCUIT BREAKER PANEL
5. ASM LOCK-UNLOCK SWITCH PANEL
6. EMERGENCY ALARM LIGHT
7. CLOCK
8. TEMPERATURE CONTROL PANEL
9. REFUEL VAVLE EMERGENCY CONTROL HANDLE
10. SPECIAL WEAPONS MANUAL LOCK HANDLE STOWAGE BRACKET
11. SPECIAL WEAPONS MANUAL LOCK HANDLE
12. CLIP BOARD STOWAGE BOX
13. INTERPHONE FOOT SWITCH
14. ASHTRAY
15. INTERPHONE CONTROL PANELS
16. OXYGEN BOTTLE RECHARGER
17. LIGHTING CONTROL PANEL
18. SPOTLIGHT
19. PORTABLE OXYGEN BOTTLE
20. ESCAPE ROPE CONTAINER
21. OXYGEN REGULATOR
22. SIDE PANEL FLOOD LIGHTS

B-52H EW OFFICER'S STATION R
TYPICAL

1. ESCAPE HATCH
2. UPPER AISLE AND ENTRY LIGHT
3. UPPER AIR OUTLET
4. ECM CIRCUIT BREAKER PANEL
5. ASM LOCK-UNLOCK SWITCH PANEL
6. EMERGENCY ALARM LIGHT
7. TEMPERATURE CONTROL PANEL
8. REFUEL VALVE EMERGENCY CONTROL HANDLE
9. SPECIAL WEAPONS MANUAL LOCK HANDLE STOWAGE BRACKET
10. SPECIAL WEAPONS MANUAL LOCK HANDLE
11. INTERPHONE FOOT SWITCH
12. INTERPHONE CONTROL PANELS
13. ASHTRAY
14. OXYGEN REGULATOR
14A. MAIN CONSOLE LIGHT CONTROL PANEL
15. PORTABLE OXYGEN BOTTLE
16. LIGHTING CONTROL PANEL
17. SPOTLIGHT
18. OXYGEN BOTTLE RECHARGER
19. ESCAPE ROPE CONTAINER
20. SIDE PANEL FLOOD LIGHTS

B-52G GUNNER'S STATION
TYPICAL

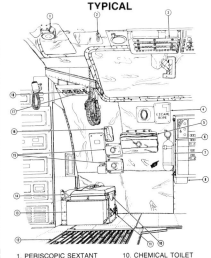

1. EMERGENCY ALARM LIGHT PANEL
2. AIR OUTLET KNOBS AND AUXILIARY HEAT KNOB
3. GUNNER'S INTERPHONE CONTROL PANEL
3A. FCS EVALUATOR SELECTOR
4. OXYGEN REGULATOR (GUNNER'S)
5. ECM CIRCUIT BREAKER PANEL
6. LINE-OF-SIGHT INDICATOR
7. TV MONITOR Less R
8. GUNNER'S STATION FLOODLIGHTS
9. AMMUNITION COUNTERS
10. Deleted
11. SPARE BULB CONTAINER
12. GUNNER'S DOMELIGHT
13. ESCAPE ROPE CONTAINER
14. GUNNER'S LIGHT CONTROL PANEL
15. GUNNER'S WARNING INDICATOR PANEL (APR-25/ALR-46)
16. FCS EXTERNAL POWER SWITCH
17. GUN CHARGER LOW PRESSURE INDICATOR LIGHT
18. FCS CIRCUIT BREAKER PANEL
18A. HOT CUP AND FOOD WARMING OVEN
19. OXYGEN RECHARGER FACILITY
19A. CABIN TEMPERATURE SENSOR BAFFLE
20. PORTABLE OXYGEN BOTTLE
21. FOOD STOWAGE BOX
22. STATION URINAL
23. FCS CONTROL PANEL
24. RADAR CONTROL PANEL
25. INTERPHONE MIKE FOOT SWITCH
26. RADAR INDICATOR
27. TV CONTROL PANEL Less R
28. GUNNER'S CONTROL HANDLE
29. REFUEL VALVE EMERGENCY CONTROL HANDLE
30. ECM SYSTEM DEACTIVATE SWITCH Less R CHAFF DEACTIVATE SWITCH R

B-52H GUNNER'S STATION
TYPICAL

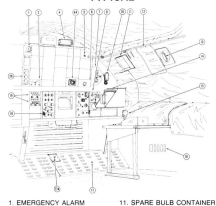

1. EMERGENCY ALARM LIGHT PANEL
2. OXYGEN REGULATOR (GUNNER'S)
3. Deleted
4. UPPER AIR OUTLET
4A. GUNNER'S WARNING INDICATOR PANEL (APR-25/ALR-46)
5. FCS EXTERNAL POWER SWITCH
6. PRESSURE SUIT FACEPLATE CONTROL PANEL
7. GUNNER'S STATION LIGHT CONTROL PANEL
8. FCS RADAR CONTROL PANEL
9. Deleted
10. GUNNER'S SPOTLIGHT
11. SPARE BULB CONTAINER
12. ESCAPE ROPE CONTAINER
13. GUNNER'S DOMELIGHT
14. HOT CUP
15. FCS MANUAL CONTROL HANDLE UNIT
16. CABIN TEMPERATURE SENSOR BAFFLE
17. GUNNER'S MICROPHONE FOOT SWITCH
17A. CHAFF DEATIVATE SWITCH
18. FCS CONTROL-INDICATOR PANEL
19. GUNNER'S INTERPHONE CONTROL PANELS
20. AIR OUTLET KNOBS AND AUXILIARY HEAT KNOB

B-52G DEFENSE INSTRUCTOR'S STATION
TYPICAL

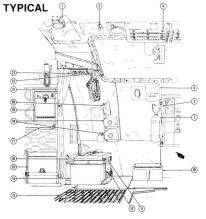

1. PERISCOPIC SEXTANT MOUNT
2. DITCHING-CRASH LANDING HAMMOCK ATTACHMENT SHACKLE
3. ECM CIRCUIT BREAKER PANEL
4. ESCAPE ROPE CONTAINER
5. BATTLE DRESSING KIT Less AA
6. PORTABLE OXYGEN RECHARGER R
7. OXYGEN BOTTLE
8. PORTABLE OXYGEN RECHARGER Less R
9. Deleted
10. CHEMICAL TOILET
11. HAND AXE
12. UPPER DECK SLIDING HATCH
13. DITCHING HAMMOCK STOWAGE
14. DEFENSE INSTRUCTOR'S SEAT
15. FIRST AID KITS
16. EMERGENCY KNIFE
17. OXYGEN REGULATOR (DEFENSE INSTRUCTOR'S)
18. DEFENSE INSTRUCTOR'S INTERPHONE CONTROL PANEL

B-52H DEFENSE INSTRUCTOR'S STATION
TYPICAL

1. PERISOPIC SEXTANT MOUNT
2. DITCHING-CRASH LANDING HAMMOCK ATTACHMENT SHACKLE
3. PORTABLE OXYGEN RECHARGER
4. ECM CIRCUIT BREAKER PANEL
5. ESCAPE ROPE CONTAINER
6. Deleted
7. OXYGEN BOTTLE
8. Deleted
9. Deleted
10. FOOD BOX
11. CHEMICAL TOILET
12. HAND AX
13. UPPER DECK SLIDING HATCH
14. DITCHING HAMMOCK STOWAGE
15. ICE BOX
16. DEFENSE INSTRUCTOR'S SEAT
17. PULL OUT TABLE
18. FIRST AID KITS
19. FOOD WARMING OVEN
20. EMERGENCY KNIFE
21. MODESTY CURTAIN
22. OXYGEN REGULATOR (DEFENSE INSTRUCTOR'S)
23. DEFENSE INSTRUCTOR'S INTERPHONE CONTROL PANEL

B-52H CREW BUNK

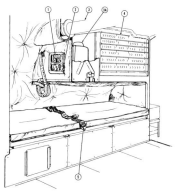

1. OXYGEN REGULATOR AND INTERPHONE
2. BUNK LIGHT SWITCH
3. CABIN MANIFOLD
3A. DRINKING WATER CONTAINER
4. LEFT LOAD CENTRAL CIRCUIT BREAKER PANEL
5. BUNK SAFETY BELT

B-52G RADAR NAVIGATOR'S STATION Less R
TYPICAL

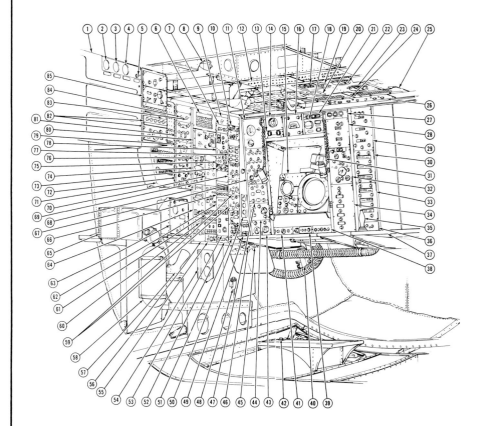

1. LEFT BNS EQUIPMENT BOX
2. COMPUTER OPERATION ELAPSE TIME METER
3. RADAR STANDBY ELAPSE TIME METER
4. RADAR RADIATE ELAPSE TIME METER
5. SERVICE DOME LIGHT SWITCH
6. BOMB INDICATOR LIGHTS
7. BNS POWER PANEL
8. COMPASS AND TRUE HEADING COMPUTER CUTOFF SWITCH
9. VGH RECORDING PANEL (INOPERATIVE)
10. IFC POWER SELECT PANEL
11. TERRAIN RADAR CONTROL PANEL
12. AFT BNS CIRCUIT BREAKER PANEL
13. BOMB DOOR CONTROL VALVE CHECK PANEL
14. BNS TEMPERATURE SENSING INDICATOR
15. TOPOCOMPT (TOPOGRAPHICAL COMPARATOR)
16. BDI (BOMBING DATA INDICATOR)
17. EXTERNAL MISSILE RELEASE SWITCHES
18. EMERGENCY ALARM LIGHT AND BNS STEERING PANEL
19. AGM-69A SELECTIVE JETTISON PANEL
20. RELEASE CIRCUITS DISCONNECT
21. BNS AIRFLOW LOW LIGHTS
22. REAR SPECIAL WEAPON MANUAL RELEASE HANDLE
23. FORWARD SPECIAL WEAPON MANUAL RELEASE HANDLE
24. LEFT FORWARD BNS CIRCUIT BREAKER PANEL
25. RIGHT FORWARD BNS CIRCUIT BREAKER PANEL
26. BNS AND AGM-69A LIGHT CONTROL PANELS
27. BNS OVERHEAT POWER SUPPLY AND RADAR LOW PRESSURE LIGHTS
28. AIRSPEED PANEL
29. LATITUDE PANEL
30. OFFSET 1 PANEL
31. RADAR RECORDING CAMERA
32. BNS DATA PRESET PANEL
33. OFFSET 2 PANEL
34. ALTITUDE PANEL
35. CROSSHAIR CONTROL
36. BNS HAND CONTROL SENSING SWITCH
37. STOWABLE WRITING TABLE
38. LOW ALTITUDE CALIBRATOR CONTROL PANEL
39. APN-150/AGM-69A TIE-IN CONTROL PANEL
40. BNS DESICCATOR
41. STC PANEL
42. INTERPHONE MIKE FOOT SWITCH
43. TARGET SCALE PANEL
44. RANGE SELECTOR PANEL
45. PRESENTATION GAIN PANEL
46. BOMB CONTROL PANEL
47. RADAR ANTENNA TILT PANEL
48. D-2 BOMB RELEASE SWITCH
49. TIME DELAY BYPASS AND BOMB TONE SCORING PANEL
50. AIR OUTLET KNOBS AND AUXILIARY HEAT KNOB
51. RADAR PRIMARY PANEL
52. AGM-69A OTL STATUS AND CONTROL PANEL
53. AGM-69A WEAPON STATUS AND CONTROL PANEL
54. BOMB INDICATOR CARDS HOLDER
55. RADAR NAVIGATOR'S INTERPHONE CONTROL PANEL
56. ADM-20 EXERCISE CONTROL PANEL
57. STATION URINAL
58. PROTABLE OXYGEN BOTTLE
59. DCU/9A CONTROL MONITOR UNITS/SWK BOXES
60. ADM-20 TRAINING PANEL
61. ADM-20 LAUNCH CONTROL PANEL
62. OXYGEN REGULATOR (RADAR NAVIGATOR'S)
63. AZIMUTH AND ELEVATION PANEL
64. ADM-20 PROGRAM PANEL
65. FOOD STOWAGE BOX
66. CODED SWITCH SET CONTROL PANEL
67. EMERGENCY CONTROLS PANEL
68. ADM-20 PROGRAM TURN PANEL
69. SPECIAL WEAPONS CONTROL PANEL
70. SPECIAL WEAPONS AND ASM LOCK INDICATOR PANEL
71. AUXILIARY BNS CIRCUIT BREAKER PANEL
72. PRESENTATION ADJUST PANEL
73. JETTISON CONTROL PANEL
74. RADAR TEST PANEL
75. BOMB RELEASE MODE CONTROL PANEL
76. TERRAIN COMPUTER POWER PANEL
77. SPECIAL WEAPONS INDICATOR LIGHTS PANEL
78. MASTER BOMB CONTROL PANEL
79. TERRAIN TEST PANEL
80. BRIC (BOMB RELEASE INTERVAL CONTROL UNIT)
81. DISPLAY PANEL (GROUND RANGE AND AZIMUTH)
82. INSTRUCTOR NAVIGATOR'S INTERPHONE CONTROL PANEL
83. GROUND BLOWERS SWITCH
84. BNS EXTERNAL POWER SWITCH
85. OXYGEN REGULATOR (INSTRUCTOR NAVIGATOR'S)

B-52H pilots' instrument panel. Major difference between G and H is the central caution panel, located by the pilot's right knee. Engine fire shutoff switches are just above engine instruments.

B-52G electronic warfare officer's station. ALR-20A panoramic scope is surrounded by transmitter controls.

B-52G RADAR NAVIGATOR'S STATION L
TYPICAL

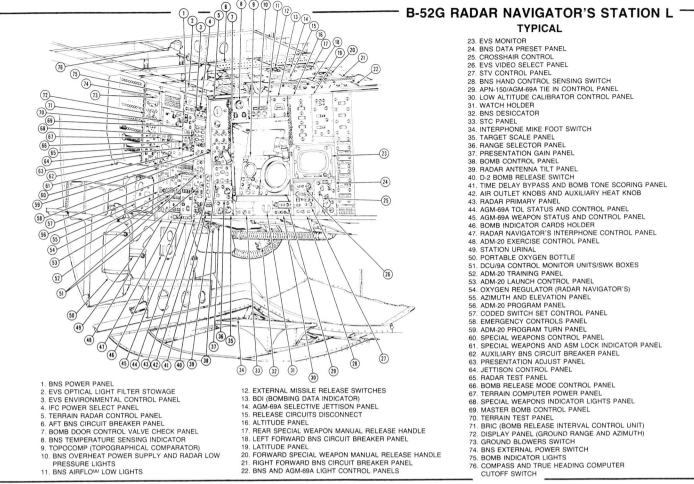

1. BNS POWER PANEL
2. EVS OPTICAL LIGHT FILTER STOWAGE
3. EVS ENVIRONMENTAL CONTROL PANEL
4. IFC POWER SELECT PANEL
5. TERRAIN RADAR CONTROL PANEL
6. AFT BNS CIRCUIT BREAKER PANEL
7. BOMB DOOR CONTROL VALVE CHECK PANEL
8. BNS TEMPERATURE SENSING INDICATOR
9. TOPOCOMP (TOPOGRAPHICAL COMPARATOR)
10. BNS OVERHEAT POWER SUPPLY AND RADAR LOW PRESSURE LIGHTS
11. BNS AIRFLOW LOW LIGHTS
12. EXTERNAL MISSILE RELEASE SWITCHES
13. BDI (BOMBING DATA INDICATOR)
14. AGM-69A SELECTIVE JETTISON PANEL
15. RELEASE CIRCUITS DISCONNECT
16. ALTITUDE PANEL
17. REAR SPECIAL WEAPON MANUAL RELEASE HANDLE
18. LEFT FORWARD BNS CIRCUIT BREAKER PANEL
19. LATITUDE PANEL
20. FORWARD SPECIAL WEAPON MANUAL RELEASE HANDLE
21. RIGHT FORWARD BNS CIRCUIT BREAKER PANEL
22. BNS AND AGM-69A LIGHT CONTROL PANELS
23. EVS MONITOR
24. BNS DATA PRESET PANEL
25. CROSSHAIR CONTROL
26. EVS VIDEO SELECT PANEL
27. STV CONTROL PANEL
28. BNS HAND CONTROL SENSING SWITCH
29. APN-150/AGM-69A TIE IN CONTROL PANEL
30. LOW ALTITUDE CALIBRATOR CONTROL PANEL
31. WATCH HOLDER
32. BNS DESICCATOR
33. STC PANEL
34. INTERPHONE MIKE FOOT SWITCH
35. TARGET SCALE PANEL
36. RANGE SELECTOR PANEL
37. PRESENTATION GAIN PANEL
38. BOMB CONTROL PANEL
39. RADAR ANTENNA TILT PANEL
40. D-2 BOMB RELEASE SWITCH
41. TIME DELAY BYPASS AND BOMB TONE SCORING PANEL
42. AIR OUTLET KNOBS AND AUXILIARY HEAT KNOB
43. RADAR PRIMARY PANEL
44. AGM-69A TOL STATUS AND CONTROL PANEL
45. AGM-69A WEAPON STATUS AND CONTROL PANEL
46. BOMB INDICATOR CARDS HOLDER
47. RADAR NAVIGATOR'S INTERPHONE CONTROL PANEL
48. ADM-20 EXERCISE CONTROL PANEL
49. STATION URINAL
50. PORTABLE OXYGEN BOTTLE
51. DCU/9A CONTROL MONITOR UNITS/SWK BOXES
52. ADM-20 TRAINING PANEL
53. ADM-20 LAUNCH CONTROL PANEL
54. OXYGEN REGULATOR (RADAR NAVIGATOR'S)
55. AZIMUTH AND ELEVATION PANEL
56. ADM-20 PROGRAM PANEL
57. CODED SWITCH SET CONTROL PANEL
58. EMERGENCY CONTROLS PANEL
59. ADM-20 PROGRAM TURN PANEL
60. SPECIAL WEAPONS CONTROL PANEL
61. SPECIAL WEAPONS AND ASM LOCK INDICATOR PANEL
62. AUXILIARY BNS CIRCUIT BREAKER PANEL
63. PRESENTATION ADJUST PANEL
64. JETTISON CONTROL PANEL
65. RADAR TEST PANEL
66. BOMB RELEASE MODE CONTROL PANEL
67. TERRAIN COMPUTER POWER PANEL
68. SPECIAL WEAPONS INDICATOR LIGHTS PANEL
69. MASTER BOMB CONTROL PANEL
70. TERRAIN TEST PANEL
71. BRIC (BOMB RELEASE INTERVAL CONTROL UNIT)
72. DISPLAY PANEL (GROUND RANGE AND AZIMUTH)
73. GROUND BLOWERS SWITCH
74. BNS EXTERNAL POWER SWITCH
75. BOMB INDICATOR LIGHTS
76. COMPASS AND TRUE HEADING COMPUTER CUTOFF SWITCH

B-52G NAVIGATOR'S STATION Less L
TYPICAL

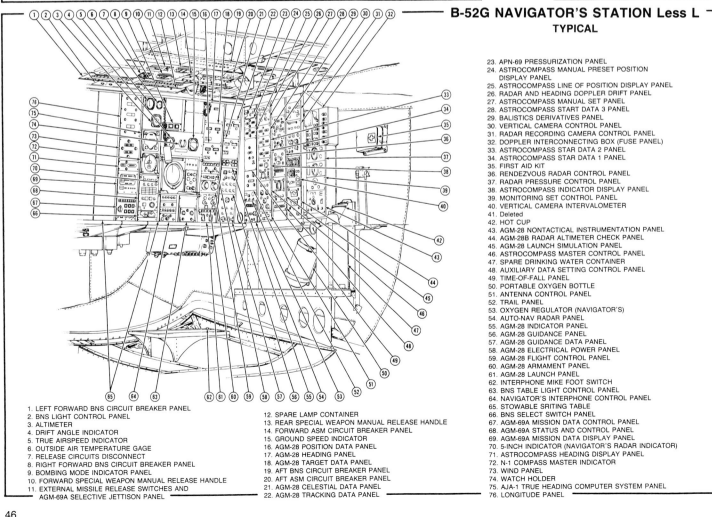

1. LEFT FORWARD BNS CIRCUIT BREAKER PANEL
2. BNS LIGHT CONTROL PANEL
3. ALTIMETER
4. DRIFT ANGLE INDICATOR
5. TRUE AIRSPEED INDICATOR
6. OUTSIDE AIR TEMPERATURE GAGE
7. RELEASE CIRCUITS DISCONNECT
8. RIGHT FORWARD BNS CIRCUIT BREAKER PANEL
9. BOMBING MODE INDICATOR PANEL
10. FORWARD SPECIAL WEAPON MANUAL RELEASE HANDLE
11. EXTERNAL MISSILE RELEASE SWITCHES AND AGM-69A SELECTIVE JETTISON PANEL
12. SPARE LAMP CONTAINER
13. REAR SPECIAL WEAPON MANUAL RELEASE HANDLE
14. FORWARD ASM CIRCUIT BREAKER PANEL
15. GROUND SPEED INDICATOR
16. AGM-28 POSITION DATA PANEL
17. AGM-28 HEADING PANEL
18. AGM-28 TARGET DATA PANEL
19. AFT BNS CIRCUIT BREAKER PANEL
20. AFT ASM CIRCUIT BREAKER PANEL
21. AGM-28 CELESTIAL DATA PANEL
22. AGM-28 TRACKING DATA PANEL
23. APN-69 PRESSURIZATION PANEL
24. ASTROCOMPASS MANUAL PRESET POSITION DISPLAY PANEL
25. ASTROCOMPASS LINE OF POSITION DISPLAY PANEL
26. RADAR AND HEADING DOPPLER DRIFT PANEL
27. ASTROCOMPASS MANUAL SET PANEL
28. ASTROCOMPASS START DATA 3 PANEL
29. BALISTICS DERIVATIVES PANEL
30. VERTICAL CAMERA CONTROL PANEL
31. RADAR RECORDING CAMERA CONTROL PANEL
32. DOPPLER INTERCONNECTING BOX (FUSE PANEL)
33. ASTROCOMPASS STAR DATA 2 PANEL
34. ASTROCOMPASS STAR DATA 1 PANEL
35. FIRST AID KIT
36. RENDEZVOUS RADAR CONTROL PANEL
37. RADAR PRESSURE CONTROL PANEL
38. ASTROCOMPASS INDICATOR DISPLAY PANEL
39. MONITORING SET CONTROL PANEL
40. VERTICAL CAMERA INTERVALOMETER
41. Deleted
42. HOT CUP
43. AGM-28 NONTACTICAL INSTRUMENTATION PANEL
44. AGM-28B RADAR ALTIMETER CHECK PANEL
45. AGM-28 LAUNCH SIMULATION PANEL
46. ASTROCOMPASS MASTER CONTROL PANEL
47. SPARE DRINKING WATER CONTAINER
48. AUXILIARY DATA SETTING CONTROL PANEL
49. TIME-OF-FALL PANEL
50. PORTABLE OXYGEN BOTTLE
51. ANTENNA CONTROL PANEL
52. TRAIL PANEL
53. OXYGEN REGULATOR (NAVIGATOR'S)
54. AUTO-NAV RADAR PANEL
55. AGM-28 INDICATOR PANEL
56. AGM-28 GUIDANCE PANEL
57. AGM-28 GUIDANCE DATA PANEL
58. AGM-28 ELECTRICAL POWER PANEL
59. AGM-28 FLIGHT CONTROL PANEL
60. AGM-28 ARMAMENT PANEL
61. AGM-28 LAUNCH PANEL
62. INTERPHONE MIKE FOOT SWITCH
63. BNS TABLE LIGHT CONTROL PANEL
64. NAVIGATOR'S INTERPHONE CONTROL PANEL
65. STOWABLE SRITING TABLE
66. BNS SELECT SWITCH PANEL
67. AGM-69A MISSION DATA CONTROL PANEL
68. AGM-69A STATUS AND CONTROL PANEL
69. AGM-69A MISSION DATA DISPLAY PANEL
70. 5-INCH INDICATOR (NAVIGATOR'S RADAR INDICATOR)
71. ASTROCOMPASS HEADING DISPLAY PANEL
72. N-1 COMPASS MASTER INDICATOR
73. WIND PANEL
74. WATCH HOLDER
75. AJA-1 TRUE HEADING COMPUTER SYSTEM PANEL
76. LONGITUDE PANEL

B-52H NAVIGATOR'S STATION L
TYPICAL

1. LEFT FORWARD BNS CIRCUIT BREAKER PANEL
2. BNS LIGHT CONTROL PANEL
3. DRIFT ANGLE INDICATOR
4. GROUND SPEED INDICATOR
5. AIRSPEED PANEL
6. ALTIMETER
7. TRUE AIRSPEED INDICATOR
8. OUTSIDE AIR TEMPERATURE GAGE
9. RELEASE CIRCUITS DISCONNECT
10. BOMBING MODE INDICATOR PANEL
11. EMERGENCY ALARM LIGHT AND BNS STEERING PANEL
12. RIGHT FORWARD BNS CIRCUIT BREAKER PANEL
13. AJN-8 PRECISE INDICATOR CONTROL PANEL
14. EXTERNAL MISSILE RELEASE SWITCHES AND AGM-69A SELECTIVE JETTISON PANEL
15. FORWARD SPECIAL WEAPON MANUAL RELEASE HANDLE
16. AGM-28 TARGET DATA PANEL
17. SPARE LAMP CONTAINER
18. REAR SPECIAL WEAPON MANUAL RELEASE HANDLE
19. FORWARD ASM CIRCUIT BREAKER PANEL
20. AGM-28 CELESTIAL DATA PANEL
21. AJN-8 SYNCHRONIZATION CONTROL PANEL
22. AJN-8 CONTROL PANEL
23. AFT BNS CIRCUIT BREAKER PANEL
24. AGM-28 HEADING PANEL
25. AFT ASM CIRCUIT BREAKER PANEL
26. AGM-28 POSITION DATA PANEL
27. AGM-28 INDICATOR LIGHTS PANEL
28. AGM-28 TRACKING DATA PANEL
29. AGM-28 ELECTRICAL POWER PANEL
30. AGM-28 FLIGHT CONTROL PANEL
31. APN-69 PRESSURIZATION PANEL
32. ASTROCOMPASS MANUAL PRESET POSITION DISPLAY PANEL
33. ASTROCOMPASS LINE OF POSITION DISPLY PANEL
34. EVS OPTICAL LIGHT FILTER STOWAGE
35. RADAR AND HEADING DOPPLER DRIFT PANEL Less R DOPPLER POWER AND DRIFT CONTROL PANEL R
36. HEADING SYSTEM CONTROL PANEL
37. ASTROCOMPASS MANUAL SET PANEL
38. J-4 HEADING SYSTEM PANEL
39. ASTROCOMPASS START DATA 3 PANEL
40. BALISTICS DERIVATIVES PANEL
41. VERTICAL CAMERA CONTROL PANEL
42. RADAR RECORDING CAMERA CONTROL PANEL
43. DOPPLER INTERCONNECTING BOX (FUSE PANEL)
44. EVS CIRCUIT BREAKER PANEL
45. ASTROCOMPASS STAR DATA 2 PANEL
46. ASTROCOMPASS STAR DATA 1 PANEL
47. FIRST AID KIT
48. RENDEZVOUS RADAR CONTROL PANEL
49. RADAR PRESSURE CONTROL PANEL
50. ASTROCOMPASS INDICATOR DISPLAY PANEL
51. MONITORING SET CONTROL PANEL
52. VERTICAL CAMERA INTERVALOMETER
53. HOT CUP
54. AGM-28 NONTACTICAL INSTRUMENTATION PANEL
55. AGM-28B RADAR ALTIMETER CHECK PANEL
56. AGM-28 LAUNCH SIMULATION PANEL
57. ASTROCOMPASS MASTER CONTROL PANEL
58. SPARE DRINKING WATER CONTAINER
59. NAVIGATOR'S INTERPHONE CONTROL PANEL
60. TIME-OF-FALL PANEL
61. PORTABLE OXYGEN BOTTLE
62. ANTENNA CONTROL PANEL
63. TRAIL PANEL
64. OXYGEN REGULATOR (NAVIGATOR'S)
65. AUTO-NAV RADAR PANEL
66. TABLE LIGHT AND EVS INDICATOR LIGHT CONTROL PANEL
67. AGM-28 ARMAMENT PANEL
68. AGM-28 LAUNCH PANEL
69. EVS VIDEO SELECT PANEL
70. EVS MONITOR
71. AGM-28 GUIDANCE PANEL
72. INTERPHONE MIKE FOOT SWITCH
73. AGM-28 GUIDANCE DATA PANEL
74. WATCH HOLDER
75. AUXILIARY DATA SETTING CONTROL PANEL Less AC
76. BNS SELECT SWITCH PANEL
77. ASTROCOMPASS HEADING DISPLAY PANEL
78. WIND PANEL
79. AGM-69A STATUS AND CONTROL PANEL
80. STOWABLE SRITING TABLE
81. EVS STEERING CONTROL PANEL
82. AGM-69A MISSION DATA CONTROL PANEL
83. AGM-69A MISSION DATA DISPLAY PANEL
84. AUTOMATED OFFSET UNIT AC OFFSET 2 PANEL Less AC
85. FLIR CONTROL PANEL
86. OFFSET 1 PANEL Less AC
87. 5-INCH INDICATOR (NAVIGATOR'S RADAR INDICATOR)
88. LONGITUDE PANEL

B-52G NAVIGATORS' COMPARTMENT-AFT L
TYPICAL

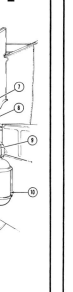

1. RIGHT SIDE REMOTE BNS MODULES
2. PRESSURE BULKHEAD DOOR
3. SERVICE DOMELIGHT
4. EMERGENCY CABIN PRESSURE RELEASE HANDLE
5. DRINKING WATER CONTAINER
6. EVS COMPONENTS
7. LEFT SIDE BNS POWER SUPPLY MODULES
8. OXYGEN REGULATOR (INSTRUCTOR NAVIGATOR'S)
9. INSTRUCTOR NAVIGATOR'S INTERPHONE CONTROL PANEL
10. PORTABLE OXYGEN BOTTLE
11. LANDING GEAR GROUND LOCK STOWAGE
12. CENTRAL URINAL
13. LOWER DECK FOLDING HATCH
14. INSTRUCTOR NAVIGATOR'S TAKEOFF AND LANDING STATION
15. LADDER
16. SPARE DRINKING WATER CONTAINER

B-52H NAVIGATORS' COMPARTMENT-AFT L
TYPICAL

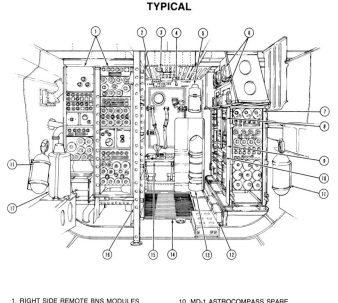

1. RIGHT SIDE REMOTE BNS MODULES
2. PRESSURE BULKHEAD DOOR
3. SERVICE DOMELIGHT
4. EMERGENCY CABIN PRESSURE RELEASE HANDLE
5. DRINKING WATER CONTAINER
6. EVS COMPONENTS
7. LEFT SIDE BNS POWER SUPPLY MODULES
8. OXYGEN REGULATOR (INSTRUCTOR NAVIGATOR'S)
9. INSTRUCTOR NAVIGATOR'S INTERPHONE CONTROL PANEL
10. MD-1 ASTROCOMPASS SPARE FUSE CONTAINER
11. PORTABLE OXYGEN BOTTLE
12. LANDING GEAR GROUND LOCK STOWAGE
13. CENTRAL URINAL
14. LOWER DECK FOLDING HATCH
15. INSTRUCTOR NAVIGATOR'S TAKEOFF AND LANDING STATION
16. LADDER
17. SPARE DRINKING WATER CONTAINER

B-52H NAVIGATORS' COMPARTMENT-AFT Less L
TYPICAL

1. RIGHT SIDE REMOTE BNS MODULE
2. PRESSURE BULKHEAD DOOR
3. EMERGENCY CABIN PRESSURE RELEASE HANDLE
3A. DRINKING WATER CONTAINER
4. LEFT BNS EQUIPMENT BOX
5. OXYGEN REGULATOR (INSTRUCTOR NAVIGATOR'S)
6. INSTRUCTOR NAVIGATOR'S INTERPHONE CONTROL PANEL
7. LEFT SIDE BNS POWER SUPPLY MODULES
8. MD-1 ASTROCOMPASS SPARE FUSE CONTAINER
9. PORTABLE OXYGEN BOTTLE
10. LANDING GEAR GROUND LOCK STOWAGE
11. CENTRAL URINAL
12. LOWER DECK FOLDING HATCH
13. INSTRUCTOR NAVIGATOR'S TAKEOFF AND LANDING STATION
14. LADDER
15. SPARE DRINKING WATER CONTAINER

B-52G EJECTION SEATS

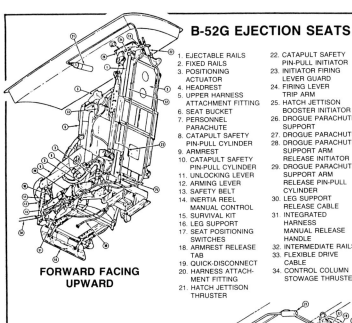

1. EJECTABLE RAILS
2. FIXED RAILS
3. POSITIONING ACTUATOR
4. HEADREST
5. UPPER HARNESS ATTACHMENT FITTING
6. SEAT BUCKET
7. PERSONNEL PARACHUTE
8. CATAPULT SAFETY PIN-PULL CYLINDER
9. ARMREST
10. CATAPULT SAFETY PIN-PULL CYLINDER
11. UNLOCKING LEVER
12. ARMING LEVER
13. SAFETY BELT
14. INERTIA REEL MANUAL CONTROL
15. SURVIVAL KIT
16. LEG SUPPORT
17. SEAT POSITIONING SWITCHES
18. ARMREST RELEASE TAB
19. QUICK-DISCONNECT
20. HARNESS ATTACHMENT FITTING
21. HATCH JETTISON THRUSTER
22. CATAPULT SAFETY PIN-PULL INITIATOR
23. INITIATOR FIRING LEVER GUARD
24. FIRING LEVER TRIP ARM
25. HATCH JETTISON BOOSTER INITIATOR
26. DROGUE PARACHUTE SUPPORT
27. DROGUE PARACHUTE SUPPORT
28. DROGUE PARACHUTE SUPPORT ARM RELEASE INITIATOR
29. DROGUE PARACHUTE SUPPORT ARM RELEASE PIN-PULL CYLINDER
30. LEG SUPPORT RELEASE CABLE
31. INTEGRATED HARNESS MANUAL RELEASE HANDLE
32. INTERMEDIATE RAILS
33. FLEXIBLE DRIVE CABLE
34. CONTROL COLUMN STOWAGE THRUSTER

FORWARD FACING UPWARD

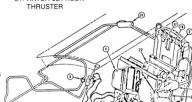

1. EJECTABLE RAILS
2. FIXED RAILS
3. POSITIONING ACTUATOR
4. HEADREST
5. UPPER HARNESS ATTACHMENT FITTING
6. SEAT BUCKET

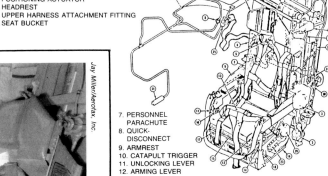

7. PERSONNEL PARACHUTE
8. QUICK-DISCONNECT
9. ARMREST
10. CATAPULT TRIGGER
11. UNLOCKING LEVER
12. ARMING LEVER
13. SAFETY BELT
14. INERTIA REE MANUAL CONTROL
15. SURVIVAL KIT
16. DRAG PANEL
17. SEAT POSITIONING SWITCHES
18. ARMREST RELEASE TAB
19. CATAPULT
20. HARNESS ATTACHMENT FITTING
21. HATCH JETTISON THRUSTER
22. MAIN-SEAT SEPARATION ACTUATOR
23. INTEGRATED HARNESS MANUAL RELEASE HANDLE
24. INTEGRATED HARNESS RELEASE ZERO DELAY INITIATOR
25. CATAPULT SAFETY PIN-PULL INITIATOR
26. MAIN-SEAT SEPARATION BOOSTER INITIATOR
27. DROGUE PARACHUTE (UNDER SEAT)
28. DRAG PANEL RELEASE CABLE
29. MAIN-SEAT SEPARATION ACTUATOR JACKSHAFT
30. INITIATOR FIRING LEVER
31. FLEXIBLE DRIVE CABLE
32. INTERMEDIATE RAILS
33. MAIN-SEAT SEPARATION HARNESS STRAPS
34. GUNNER FIRE CONTROL SUPPORT STOWAGE THRUSTER

AFT FACING UPWARD

DOWNWARD EJECTION SYSTEM

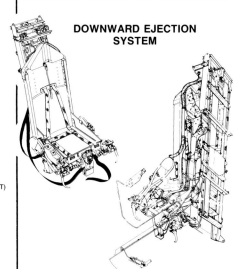

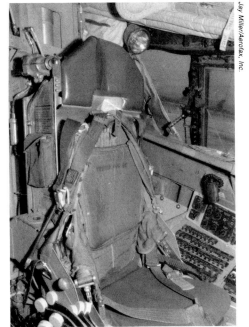

B-52G pilot's ejection seat. Weber seat uses 0.75 sec. 'chute in integrated harness arrangement.

B-52H copilot's ejection seat. B-52 pilots must step over aisle stand to climb into seats.

B-52G ESCAPE HATCHES

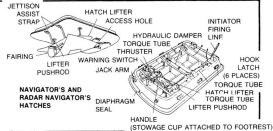

B-52G ENTRANCE TO AIRCRAFT

B-52G gunner's station. FCS radar and turret control slides out from panel for use; stows for egress.

B-52H gunner's station. Tracking handle at right is used to move the radar antennas and the cannon.

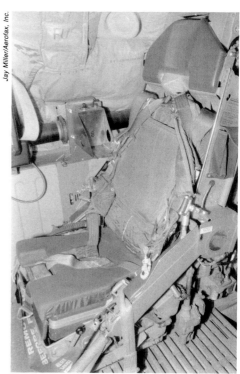
B-52H gunner's ejection seat is virtually identical to pilots'. Hot cup mount is by gunner's shoulder.

B-52H crew bunk and "10th man" position. Ditching hammock is used as a backrest for 10th man.

B-52H aisle area showing left and right load central circuit breaker panels, crew bunk, night flying curtain, and instructor pilot's seat. "Dinner table" unique to B-52H is at far right.

B-52G nose section shows window arrangement, including copilot's hatch window. Thermal curtains can be seen in their stowed positions.

B-52G radar navigator's (left) and navigator's (right) forward panels. Each has two multifunctional displays (MFDs) and an integrated keyboard (IKB).

B-52H radar navigator's station. Radar navigator management panel dominates forward part of station.

Center part of RN/N position. Various panels control FLIR/STV and data transfer unit cartridge loading.

B-52H navigator's station, with strike camera control, Doppler, and rendezvous beacon panels.

B-52G/H crew entrance door. Door may be closed from inside or outside but is locked only from inside.

Area aft of navigators' station, showing instructor navigator seat, urinal, and OAS equipment racks.

Contours of EVS and ALQ-117 antenna fairings and position of landing lights and crew entry door.

Pre-EVS nose contour of B-52G, 57-6498, provides view of original radome.

EVS-equipped B-52H nose contour differs considerably from that of the aircraft as originally built.

Open STV turret reveals camera and mirror assembly. Camera is mounted vertically.

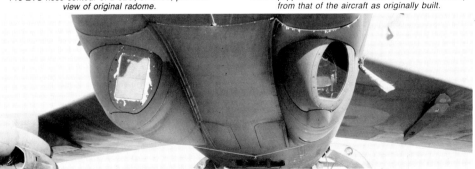
EVS installation on the B-52G/H features FLIR on the aircraft right side and STV on the left. The cameras can be rotated 45 degrees either side of the nose. The germanium FLIR window is opaque.

Distinctive features of the ALCM B-52G include rounded wing roots referred to as strakelets, and 31 small vortex generators near upper wing leading edges.

Strakelet fairing includes a slightly modified cooling air inlet scoop. Various air conditioning exhaust vents are on the left fuselage side.

Seven spoiler segments on each wing work in inboard and outboard "groups." Fifty vortex generators are located on the inboard upper wing area.

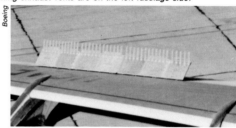
Airbrake "fences" parallel wing airflow and are hinged accordingly. Actuation is hydraulic.

Left inboard flap segment. Flaps rotate downward to full 35° in first 37.5% of extension sequence.

Trailing portion of flap serves as wing upper surface when flaps are retracted.

Left outboard flap segment. Segment's two jackscrews are driven by electric motors via a torque tube.

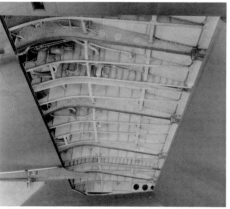
Wing rib structure and miscellaneous plumbing are visible inside left inboard flap well.

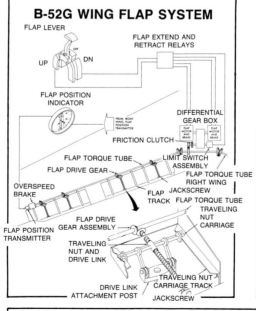

B-52G WING FLAP SYSTEM

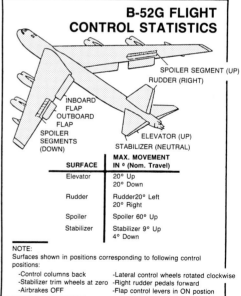

B-52G FLIGHT CONTROL STATISTICS

SURFACE	MAX. MOVEMENT IN ° (Nom. Travel)
Elevator	20° Up / 20° Down
Rudder	Rudder 20° Left / 20° Right
Spoiler	Spoiler 60° Up
Stabilizer	Stabilizer 9° Up / 4° Down

NOTE:
Surfaces shown in positions corresponding to following control positions:
- Control columns back
- Stabilizer trim wheels at zero
- Airbrakes OFF
- Lateral control wheels rotated clockwise
- Right rudder pedals forward
- Flap control levers in ON position

EVS MAJOR COMPONENTS

EVS RELAYS AND CONTROLLERS
STV CAMERA ELECTRONICS
FLIR SIGNAL PROCESSOR
BNS RADAR MODULATOR (REFERENCE)
BNS RADAR RECEIVER-TRANSMITTER (REFERENCE)
FLIR SCANNER ASSEMBLY
FLIR TURRET DRIVE
FLIR TURRET
STV TURRET DRIVE
STV CAMERA ASSEMBLY
STV TURRET
NOSE RADOME

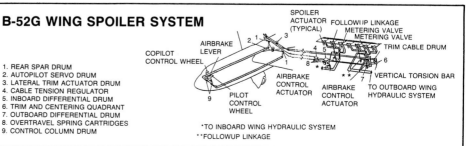

B-52G WING SPOILER SYSTEM

1. REAR SPAR DRUM
2. AUTOPILOT SERVO DRUM
3. LATERAL TRIM ACTUATOR DRUM
4. CABLE TENSION REGULATOR
5. INBOARD DIFFERENTIAL DRUM
6. TRIM AND CENTERING QUADRANT
7. OUTBOARD DIFFERENTIAL DRUM
8. OVERTRAVEL SPRING CARTRIDGES
9. CONTROL COLUMN DRUM

*TO INBOARD WING HYDRAULIC SYSTEM
**FOLLOWUP LINKAGE

B-52G/H wingtips are reinforced fiberglass. Scoop is for fuel surge tank pressurization.

B-52A, 52-001, served as Boeing's testbed for the B-52G/H shortened vertical tail surfaces. This configuration verified directional stability attributes that had been predicted by Boeing engineers.

ASG-15 FCS radar and aft ALQ-117 system components are located above the turret on the B-52G. ALQ-153 TWS fairing is on the vertical fin.

The same ALQ-117 components are located in small blisters above and below the B-52H cannon. Rounded fairing at base of fin houses ALQ-172(V)2 antenna.

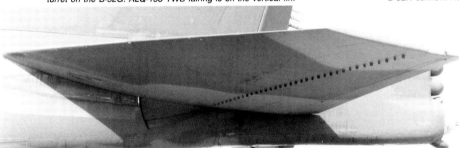

Thirty five vortex generators on the upper and lower surfaces of the horizontal stabilizer provide airflow control across the 10 percent chord elevator. The entire stabilizer is rotated for pitch trim.

Canister on inside of drag chute door holds the 44-foot diameter ribbon parachute.

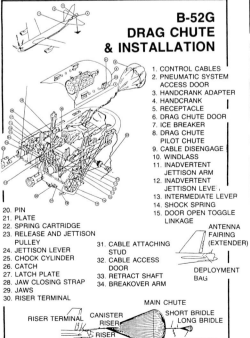

B-52G DRAG CHUTE & INSTALLATION

1. CONTROL CABLES
2. PNEUMATIC SYSTEM ACCESS DOOR
3. HANDCRANK ADAPTER
4. HANDCRANK
5. RECEPTACLE
6. DRAG CHUTE DOOR
7. ICE BREAKER
8. DRAG CHUTE PILOT CHUTE
9. CABLE DISENGAGE
10. WINDLASS
11. INADVERTENT JETTISON ARM
12. INADVERTENT JETTISON LEVER
13. INTERMEDIATE LEVER
14. SHOCK SPRING
15. DOOR OPEN TOGGLE LINKAGE
20. PIN
21. PLATE
22. SPRING CARTRIDGE
23. RELEASE AND JETTISON PULLEY
24. JETTISON LEVER
25. CHOCK CYLINDER
26. CATCH
27. LATCH PLATE
28. JAW CLOSING STRAP
29. JAWS
30. RISER TERMINAL
31. CABLE ATTACHING STUD
32. CABLE ACCESS DOOR
33. RETRACT SHAFT
34. BREAKOVER ARM

Crosswind landing and taxi lights are mounted on the right forward gear strut; landing light is on door.

Right forward gear rotates clockwise and retracts aft into gear well.

Left forward gear rotates clockwise and forward for retraction.

Indentation for tire clearance is much larger on the right aft gear door

Left forward gear well contains aircraft battery boxes and numerous power distribution panels.

Air conditioning system components occupy considerable space in the left forward wheel well.

Main landing gear retract in 10 to 15 seconds; extend in 15 to 20 seconds.

Up to 20 degrees of crosswind crab steering position may be set on the aft trucks.

Landing gear struts and actuators share space in the right forward gear well with various power boxes.

Air conditioning plumbing, wiring harnesses, and power boxes are visible in the top of the left forward well.

Right aft wheel well is very uncluttered. Four spare starter cartridges may be carried on the ledge.

Left aft gear extension and retraction is identical to that for the left forward gear.

Inner surface of left forward gear door has a small indentation to fit around tires when closed.

Right aft gear well is considerably less "busy" than the forward wells.

A body system standby hydraulic pump is located in the left aft wheel well.

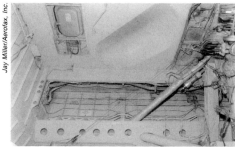
Indentation in the right aft gear well for the tire is noteworthy as are flight control cables.

53

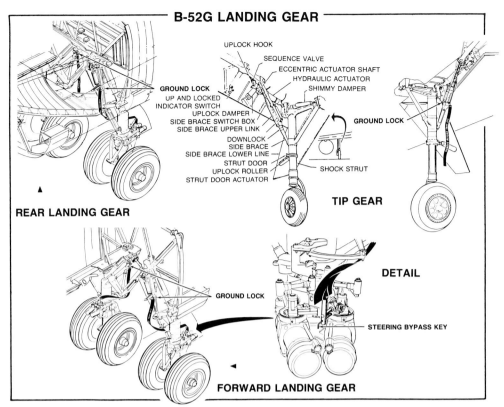

The tip gears receive hydraulic power from the #1 and #7 engine hydraulic systems, respectively.

The outboard tip gear door is attached to the strut. Strut compression depends on fuel weight in wing.

Tip gear actuator arm and strut detail. Tip gear retracts inboard approximately parallel to the wing MAC.

The wheel well door opens first and closes last in the tip gear operating sequence.

Outrigger wheel and tire assembly are rigidly attached to gear strut.

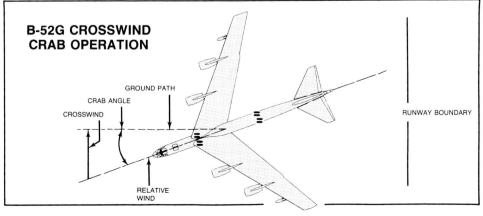

The inboard tip gear door has a separate hydraulic actuator, and covers the tire when retracted.

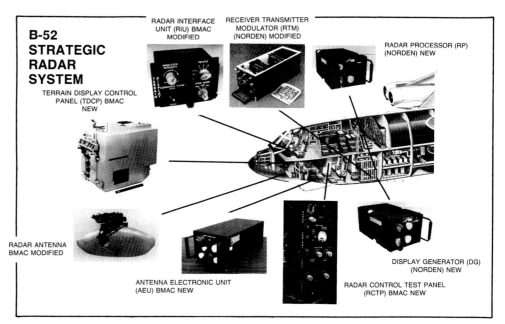

B-52 STRATEGIC RADAR SYSTEM

- TERRAIN DISPLAY CONTROL PANEL (TDCP) BMAC NEW
- RADAR INTERFACE UNIT (RIU) BMAC MODIFIED
- RECEIVER TRANSMITTER MODULATOR (RTM) (NORDEN) MODIFIED
- RADAR PROCESSOR (RP) (NORDEN) NEW
- RADAR ANTENNA BMAC MODIFIED
- ANTENNA ELECTRONIC UNIT (AEU) BMAC NEW
- DISPLAY GENERATOR (DG) (NORDEN) NEW
- RADAR CONTROL TEST PANEL (RCTP) BMAC NEW

Open fairing on B-52H 60-0004 ("UPDRAFT") shows ALQ-117 antenna "horns." STV turret housing is removed showing positioning of camera assembly.

Detail of ECM racks and OAS ground mapping radar underneath nose radome. Locking braces hold the radome up when it is opened for maintenance activity. (Brian Rogers)

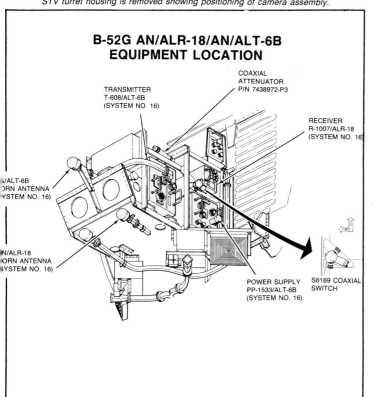

B-52G AN/ALR-18/AN/ALT-6B EQUIPMENT LOCATION

- TRANSMITTER T-608/ALT-6B (SYSTEM NO. 16)
- COAXIAL ATTENUATOR P/N 7438972-P3
- RECEIVER R-1007/ALR-18 (SYSTEM NO. 16)
- /ALT-6B ORN ANTENNA YSTEM NO. 16)
- N/ALR-18 ORN ANTENNA SYSTEM NO. 16)
- POWER SUPPLY PP-1533/ALT-6B (SYSTEM NO. 16)
- S6169 COAXIAL SWITCH

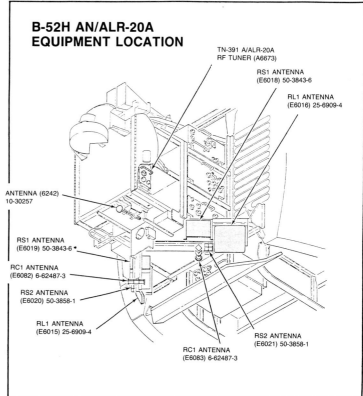

B-52H AN/ALR-20A EQUIPMENT LOCATION

- TN-391 A/ALR-20A RF TUNER (A6673)
- RS1 ANTENNA (E6018) 50-3843-6
- RL1 ANTENNA (E6016) 25-6909-4
- ANTENNA (6242) 10-30257
- RS1 ANTENNA (E6019) 50-3843-6
- RC1 ANTENNA (E6082) 6-62487-3
- RS2 ANTENNA (E6020) 50-3858-1
- RL1 ANTENNA (E6015) 25-6909-4
- RC1 ANTENNA (E6083) 6-62487-3
- RS2 ANTENNA (E6021) 50-3858-1

AN/ALQ-155 ECM antenna farm is located underneath the forward fuselage, just ahead of the main landing gear wells.

Alert B-52H at Minot AFB (circa 1972), loaded with AGM-28B "Hound Dog" missiles and ALE-25 forward-firing chaff rockets. Pre-EVS nose.

Extended B-52H empennage section is mounting location for AN/ALQ-117 aft antenna horn fairing and RHAW antenna. Noteworthy are numerous access panels for ECM and FCS equipment.

Miscellaneous ECM antenna and cooling air exhaust ports on aft fuselage underside area.

Protective covers for the ALE-20 flare bays, which are located on the lower surface of the stabilizers.

Though the quality is poor, this photo apparently depicts an ALQ-119 ECM pod loaded on the right wing chaff rocket hard point. Unconfirmed reports exist of combat use of ALQ-119 on Guam B-52G's.

B-52G AN/ALR-20A EQUIPMENT LOCATION

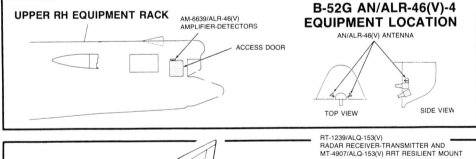
UPPER RH EQUIPMENT RACK

B-52G AN/ALR-46(V)-4 EQUIPMENT LOCATION

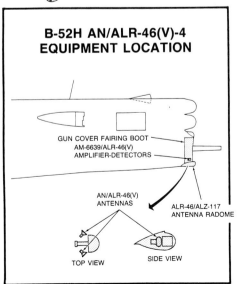
B-52H AN/ALR-46(V)-4 EQUIPMENT LOCATION

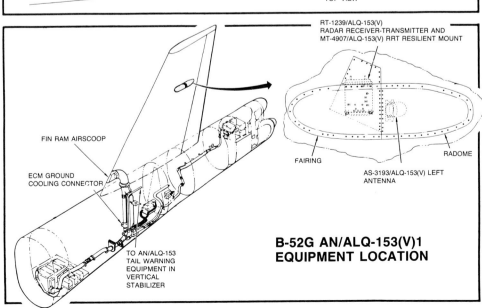
B-52G AN/ALQ-153(V)1 EQUIPMENT LOCATION

56

B-52G ECM ANTENNA LOCATION

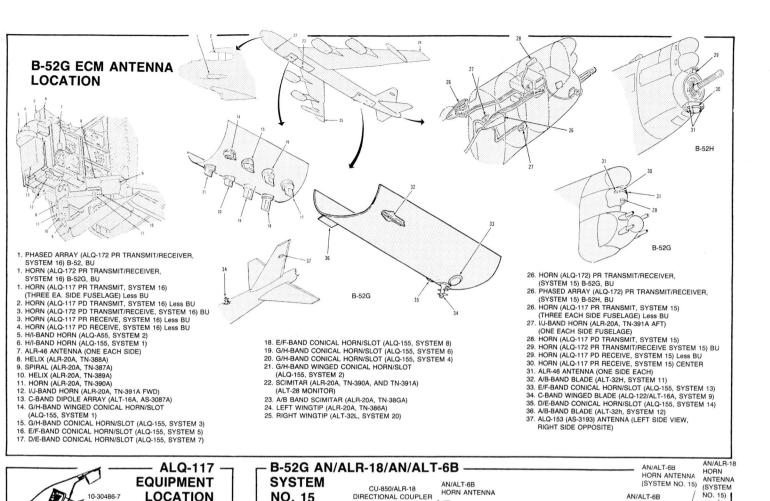

1. PHASED ARRAY (ALQ-172 PR TRANSMIT/RECEIVER, SYSTEM 16) B-52, BU
1. HORN (ALQ-172 PR TRANSMIT/RECEIVER, SYSTEM 16) B-52G, BU
1. HORN (ALQ-117 PR TRANSMIT, SYSTEM 16) (THREE EA. SIDE FUSELAGE) Less BU
2. HORN (ALQ-117 PD TRANSMIT, SYSTEM 16) Less BU
3. HORN (ALQ-172 PD TRANSMIT/RECEIVE, SYSTEM 16) BU
3. HORN (ALQ-117 PR RECEIVE, SYSTEM 16) Less BU
4. HORN (ALQ-117 PD RECEIVE, SYSTEM 16) Less BU
5. H/I-BAND HORN (ALQA55, SYSTEM 2)
6. H/I-BAND HORN (ALQ-155, SYSTEM 1)
7. ALR-46 ANTENNA (ONE EACH SIDE)
8. HELIX (ALR-20A, TN-388A)
9. SPIRAL (ALR-20A, TN-387A)
10. HELIX (ALR-20A, TN-389A)
11. HORN (ALR-20A, TN-390A)
12. I/J-BAND HORN (ALR-20A, TN-391A FWD)
13. C-BAND DIPOLE ARRAY (ALT-16A, AS-3087A)
14. G/H-BAND WINGED CONICAL HORN/SLOT (ALQ-155, SYSTEM 1)
15. G/H-BAND CONICAL HORN/SLOT (ALQ-155, SYSTEM 3)
16. E/F-BAND CONICAL HORN/SLOT (ALQ-155, SYSTEM 5)
17. D/E-BAND CONICAL HORN/SLOT (ALQ-155, SYSTEM 7)
18. E/F-BAND CONICAL HORN/SLOT (ALQ-155, SYSTEM 8)
19. G/H-BAND CONICAL HORN/SLOT (ALQ-155, SYSTEM 6)
20. G/H-BAND CONICAL HORN/SLOT (ALQ-155, SYSTEM 4)
21. G/H-BAND WINGED CONICAL HORN/SLOT (ALQ-155, SYSTEM 2)
22. SCIMITAR (ALR-20A, TN-390A, AND TN-391A) (ALT-28 MONITOR)
23. A/B BAND SCIMITAR (ALR-20A, TN-38GA)
24. LEFT WINGTIP (ALR-20A, TN-386A)
25. RIGHT WINGTIP (ALT-32L, SYSTEM 20)
26. HORN (ALQ-172) PR TRANSMIT/RECEIVER, (SYSTEM 15) B-52G, BU
26. PHASED ARRAY (ALQ-172) PR TRANSMIT/RECEIVER, (SYSTEM 15) B-52H, BU
26. HORN (ALQ-117 PR TRANSMIT, SYSTEM 15) (THREE EACH SIDE FUSELAGE) Less BU
27. I/J-BAND HORN (ALR-20A, TN-391A AFT) (ONE EACH SIDE FUSELAGE)
28. HORN (ALQ-117 PD TRANSMIT, SYSTEM 15)
29. HORN (ALQ-172 PR TRANSMIT/RECEIVE SYSTEM 15) BU
29. HORN (ALQ-117 PD RECEIVE, SYSTEM 15) Less BU
30. HORN (ALQ-117 PR RECEIVE, SYSTEM 15) CENTER
31. ALR-46 ANTENNA (ONE SIDE EACH)
32. A/B-BAND BLADE (ALT-32H, SYSTEM 11)
33. E/F-BAND CONICAL HORN/SLOT (ALQ-155, SYSTEM 13)
34. C-BAND WINGED BLADE (ALQ-122/ALT-16A, SYSTEM 9)
35. D/E-BAND CONICAL HORN/SLOT (ALQ-155, SYSTEM 14)
36. A/B-BAND BLADE (ALT-32h, SYSTEM 12)
37. ALQ-153 (AS-3193) ANTENNA (LEFT SIDE VIEW, RIGHT SIDE OPPOSITE)

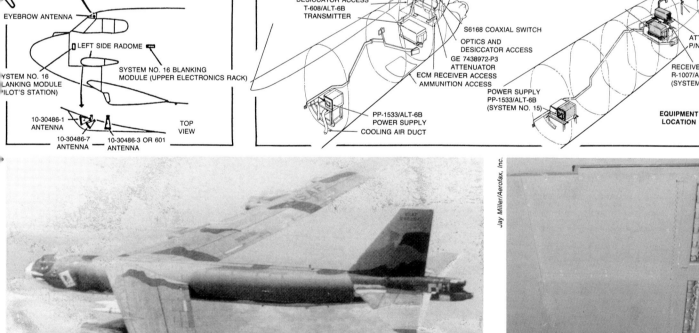

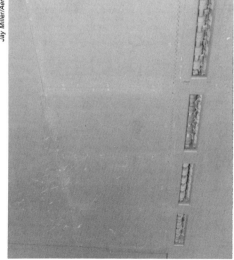

B-52G, 58-0204 was the testbed for "Rivet Ace" ECM modifications. Noteworthy is the antenna fairing on the left horizontal stabilizer, believed to be a trial mount for the ALQ-153 TWS.

Four chaff bays are located on the underside of each wing between the flap segments.

57

B-52G ANTENNA LOCATIONS
(Except ECM)

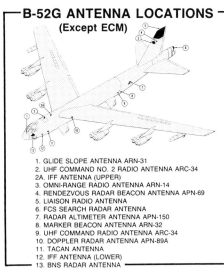

1. GLIDE SLOPE ANTENNA ARN-31
2. UHF COMMAND NO. 2 RADIO ANTENNA ARC-34
2A. IFF ANTENNA (UPPER)
3. OMNI-RANGE RADIO ANTENNA ARN-14
4. RENDEZVOUS RADAR BEACON ANTENNA APN-69
5. LIAISON RADIO ANTENNA
6. FCS SEARCH RADAR ANTENNA
7. RADAR ALTIMETER ANTENNA APN-150
8. MARKER BEACON ANTENNA ARN-32
9. UHF COMMAND RADIO ANTENNA ARC-34
10. DOPPLER RADAR ANTENNA APN-89A
11. TACAN ANTENNA
12. IFF ANTENNA (LOWER)
13. BNS RADAR ANTENNA

B-52 DEFENSIVE AVIONICS SYSTEMS

	56	57	58	59	60	61	62	63	64	65	66	67	68	69	70-84	85
	0			I			II/III		IV			V			VI	Follow-On
Sensors	APR-9 APR-14 APS-54			APR-9 APR-14 APS-54			APR-9 APR-14 APR-54 ALR-18		APR-9 APR-25 ALR-18			ALR-20 APR-25 ALR-18			ALR-20 ALR-46 ALQ-117 ALQ-122 ALQ-155 ALQ-153	ALR-20 ALQ-172V (I) (G) ALQ-172V (II) (H) CSA ECM
Jammers	14 ALT-6B			10 ALT-6B 2 ALT-13 1 ALT-15H 1 ALT-16			5 ALT-6B 2 ALT-13 2 ALT-15H 1 ALT-15L 1 ALT-16		5 ALT-6B 2 ALT-13 2 ALT-15H 1 ALT-15L 1 ALT-16			4 ALT-6B 6 ALT-28 2 ALT-32H 1 ALT-32L 2 ALT-16			10 ALQ-155 2 ALT-32H 1 ALT-32L 2 ALT-16 4 ALQ-117 1 ALQ-122 1 ALQ-153	ALQ-172V (I) (G) ALQ-172V (II) (H) CSA ECM
Chaff	2 ALE-1			2 ALE-1			8 ALE-24		8 ALE-24 2 ALE-25			8 ALE-24 2 ALE-25			8 ALE-24	
Flares							6 ALE-20		6 ALE-20			6 ALE-20			12 ALE-20	

B-52H ANTENNA LOCATIONS
(Except ECM)

1. GLIDE SLOPE ANTENNA ARN-31
2. NO. 2 UHG COMMAND RADIO ANTENNA
2A. IFF ANTENNA (UPPER)
3. OMNI-RANGE RADIO ANTENNA ARN-14
4. RENDEZVOUS RADAR BEACON ANTENNA APN-69
5. LIAISON RADIO ANTENNA ARC-58
6. FCS SEARCH RADAR ANTENNAS
6A. RADAR ALTIMETER ANTENNA APN-150
7. MARKER BEACON ANTENNA ARN-32
8. NO. 1 UHF COMMAND RADIO ANTENNA
9. DOPPLER RADAR ANTENNA APN-89A
10. TACAN ANTENNA
11. IFF ANTENNA (LOWER) FLUSH
12. RADAR BOMBING-NAVIGATIONS SYSTEM ANTENNA

B-62G/H OFFENSIVE AVIONICS SYSTEM

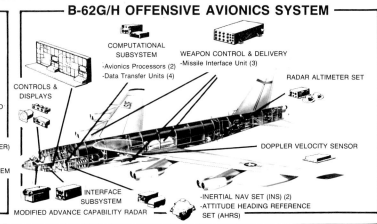

B-52G COMMUNICATION AND ASSOCIATED ELECTRONIC EQUIPMENT

TYPE	DESIGNATION	FUNCTION	OPERATOR	HORIZONTAL RANGE	LOCATION OF CONTROLS
INTERPHONE	AN/AIC-10A	Intercrew communication	Any crew member		Each crew station
UHF COMMAND	AN/ARC-34	Short range, two-way voice and code communication	Pilot and Copilot	75 to 270 miles	Pilots' overhead panel
UHF COMMAND NO. 2	AN/ARC-34				
LIAISON RADIO	AN/ARC-65 [W172] [W180] AN/ARC-58 [W181]	Long range, two-way voice and code communication	Copilot	800 to 1500 miles	Copilot's side panel
TACAN RADIO	AN/ARN-21	UHF navigation	Pilot and Copilot	195 miles	Pilots' overhead panel
OMNI RANGE RADIO	AN/ARN-14	Indicates lateral alignment with runway and used for VHF navigation	Pilot and Copilot	Line of Sight	Pilots' overhead panel
GLIDE SLOPE	AN/ARN-31	Indicates glide angle for landing	Pilot and Copilot	15 miles	Operates through omni range radio
MARKER BEACON	AN/ARN-32	Receives location marker signals on navigation beam	Pilot and Copilot	Low altitude	Operates through omni range radio
RADAR ALTIMETER	AN/APN-150	Measures terrain clearance	Pilot		Pilots' instrument panel
RENDEZVOUS RADAR	AN/APN-69	Aerial rendezvous	Navigator	150 to 200 miles	Navigator's side panel
IFF RADAR	AN/APX-64	Aircraft recognition, IFF Mode 4	Pilot	Line of Sight	Pilot's side panel
N-1 COMPASS SYSTEM		Provides heading reference	Navigator		Navigator's station
BNS RADAR (COMPONENT OF AN/ASQ-38(V))		Provides bombing, navigation, and low level flight assist	Pilot, Copilot, and Radar Navigator		Pilot, copilot, and radar navigator's station
AUTOMATIC ASTROCOMPASS SYSTEM (COMPONENT OF AN/ASQ-38(V))	MD-1	Provides heading reference	Navigator		Navigator's station
AJA-1 TRUE HEADING COMPUTER SYSTEM (COMPONENT OF AN/ASQ-38(V))	AN/AJA-1	Provides heading reference	Navigator		Navigator's station
DOPPLER RADAR (COMPONENT OF AN/ASQ-38(V))	AN/APN-89A	Ground speed and wind drift	Navigator		Navigator's side panel
BOMBING NAVIGATION SYSTEM (COMPONENT OF AN/ASQ-38(V))	AN/ASB-16	Bombing and navigation	Radar Navigator		Radar navigator's station
ELECTRO-OPTICAL VIEWING SYSTEM EVS [L]	AN/ASQ-151	Low level flight assist	Pilot, Copilot, Radar Navigator and Navigator	Line of Sight	Pilot, copilot, radar navigator, and navigator's stations
FIRE CONTROL SYSTEM	AN/ASG-15	Fire control	Gunner		Gunner's station

B-52G AN/ALE-24 EQUIPMENT LOCATION

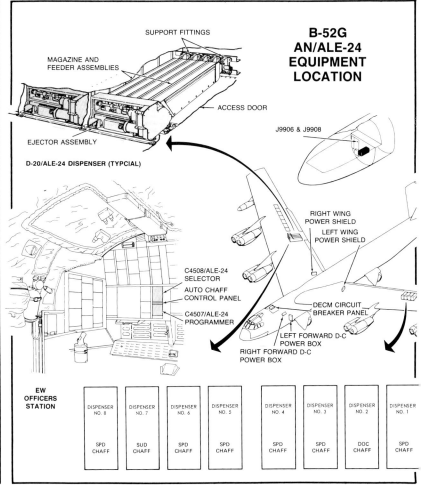

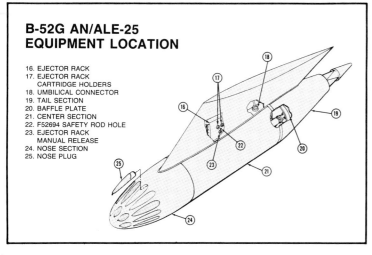

B-52G AN/ALE-25 EQUIPMENT LOCATION

16. EJECTOR RACK
17. EJECTOR RACK CARTRIDGE HOLDERS
18. UMBILICAL CONNECTOR
19. TAIL SECTION
20. BAFFLE PLATE
21. CENTER SECTION
22. F52694 SAFETY ROD HOLE
23. EJECTOR RACK MANUAL RELEASE
24. NOSE SECTION
25. NOSE PLUG

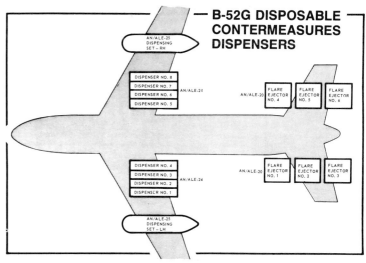

B-52G DISPOSABLE COUNTERMEASURES DISPENSERS

B-52G engine nacelle features ram air scoops for engine oil cooling and cooling of the constant speed drives (CSDs).

B-52G engine side cowlings open for maintenance. Support rods secure the cowl segments, allowing work access without removal.

Bleed-air for air conditioning and pressurization is taken from the #3 and #4 engines. The #2 pod strut differs from the other three in having an exhaust duct for the bleed air system.

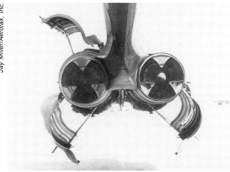

Three sonic suppressors are mounted in the exhaust ducts on J57-P-43WB engines to reduce sonic vibration.

Plumbing on the #8 engine of a B-52G. Engines #2 and do not operate hydraulic packs or generators.

The hydraulic pump is installed on the lower right side; AC generator on the lower left side of all four odd-numbered engines.

B-52H/TF33-P-3 inlet. No cooling air ducts are found on the TF33. Engine oil is cooled by means of a fuel-oil cooler (heat exchange) system.

Turbofan bypass air exits out the fan air bypass ducts, which do not wrap around the entire circumference of the nacelles.

Nose, ring, and wrap cowls are commonly swapped between airplanes at B-52H units, thus explaining the paint pattern 'mismatch' seen on the #8 engine in this photo.

B-52H engine nacelles are suspended by pylon assemblies that are different from B-52G's.

First two compressor stages comprise TF33 fan section. Fan ducting routes air around aft section which contains burner section and exhaust nozzle.

TF33 engine accessories are driven from an accessories gearbox by a shaft mechanically geared to the main turbine shaft.

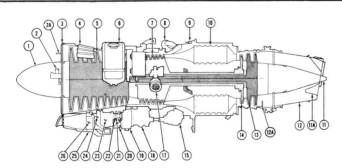

B-52G ENGINE TYPE J-57-P-43WB

1. NOSE DOME
2. SURGE BLEED VALVE GOVERNOR
2A. EPR PROBE (INLET PRESSURE)
3. NOSE COWL SEAT
4. IGNITION UNITS
5. LOW PRESSURE COMPRESSOR
6. OIL TANK, ENGINE
7. HIGHT PRESSURE COMPRESSOR
8. BLEED AIR DUCT
9. FIRE DETECTOR
10. BURNER CANS
11. EXHAUST CONE
11A. SONIC VIBRATION SUPPRESSORS
12. TAILPIPE
12A. EPR PROBE (EXHAUST PRESSURE)
13. 2ND AND 3RD STAGE TURBINES
14. 1ST STAGE TURBINE
15. ACCESSORY DRIVE
16. Deleted
17. SURGE BLEED VALVE
18. FUEL CONTROL UNIT
19. ACCESSORY DRIVE CASE
20. STARTER
21. ENGINE-DRIVEN HYDRAULIC PUMP
22. ENGINE-DRIVEN WATER PUMP
23. CONSTANT SPEED DRIVE UNIT
24. A-C GENERATOR
25. OIL COOLER, ENGINE
26. OIL COOLER, GENERATOR CS DRIVE

ENGINE DRIVEN ACCESSORIES

ENGINE NO.	1	2	3	4	5	6	7	8
HYDRAULIC PUMP	✓		✓	✓	✓	✓	✓	
WATER PUMP		✓		✓		✓		✓
A C GENERATOR & CONSTANT SPEED DRIVE	✓			✓		✓		✓

ENGINES	THRUST IN POUNDS AT SEA LEVEL NACA STANDARD DAY			MATERIAL
	TAKEOFF RATED THRUST WITH WATER INJECTION	MILITARY RATED THRUST (NO WATER)	NORMAL RATED THRUST	
J-57-P-43WB	13,750	11,200	9,500	TITANIUM

J-57-P-43WB engines are flat rated to develop "wet" takeoff thrust at sea level conditions other than an NACA standard day.

B-52H ENGINE TYPE TF33-P-3

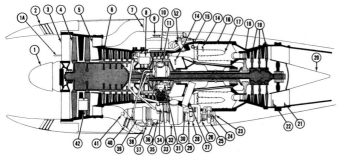

1. NOSE DOME
1A. EPR PROBE (INLET PRESSURE)
2. AUXILIARY AIR INLET DOORS
3. INLET GUIDE VANES
4. LOW PRESSURE COMPRESSOR, FAN STAGES
5. FAN AIR EXIT VANES
6. LOW PRESSURE COMPRESSOR, BLADE STAGES
7. FAN AIR DUCT EXIT
8. FUEL STRAINER
9. OIL TANK, ENGINE
10. HIGH PRESSURE COMPRESSOR
11. OIL TANK, CONSTANT SPEED DRIVE
12. BLEED AIR DUCT
13. Deleted
14. FIRE DETECTORS (ON ENGINE FIREWALL)
15. FUEL MANIFOLD (DUAL)
16. COMBUSTION CHAMBER
17. COMBUSTION CHAMBER CENTER TUBE
18. FIRST STAGE TURBINE
19. 2ND, 3RD, AND 4TH STAGE TURBINES
20. EXHAUST CONE
21. EGT PROBE
22. EPR PROBE (EXHAUST PRESSURE)
23. FIRE SEAL
24. FUEL-OIL COOLER
25. FUEL FLOWMETER
26. PRESSURIZING AND DUMP VALVE
27. ACCESSORY DRIVE
28. STARTER
29. HYDRAULIC PUMP
30. TACHOMETER GENERATOR
31. SURGE BLEED VALVE ACTUATOR AND GOVERNOR
32. ACCESSORY DRIVE CASE
33. SURGE BLEED VALVE PORT
34. FUEL PUMP
35. CONSTANT SPEED DRIVE
36. FUEL CONTROL UNIT
37. GENERATOR COOLING AIR OUTLET
38. CSD OIL COOLER AIR OUTLET
39. A-C GENERATOR
40. CSD OIL COOLER
41. GENERATOR COOL AIR INLET
42. IGNITION UNIT

ENGINE DRIVEN ACCESSORIES

ENGINE NO.	1	2	3	4	5	6	7	8
HYDRAULIC PUMP	✓		✓	✓	✓	✓	✓	
A C GENERATOR & CONSTANT SPEED DRIVE	✓		✓		✓		✓	

ENGINES	THRUST IN POUNDS AT SEA LEVEL ICAO STANDARD DAY			MATERIAL
	TAKEOFF RATED THRUST	MILITARY RATED THRUST	NORMAL RATED THRUST	
TF33-P-3	17,000	16,500	14,500	TITANIUM

Generator and constant speed drive for odd-numbered engines (1, 3, 5, 7) are mounted on the bottom centerline of the engine near the fan exhaust duct.

Fixed 700 US gallon external tanks are found on all B-52G/H aircraft. Only one boost pump is needed in each tank, as wing flex provides some gravity feed.

B-52G/H FUEL QUANTITY DATA

TANK CAPACITIES

TANKS	NO.	USABLE FUEL (EACH)		FULLY SERVICED (EACH)	
		POUNDS	GALLONS	POUNDS	GALLONS
NO. 1 & 4 MAIN	2	31,843	4,899	31,883	4,905
NO. 2 & 3 MAIN	2	44,259	6,809	44,421	6,834
MID BODY	1	46,410	7,140	46,501	7,154
FORWARD BODY	1	13,319	2,049	13,345	2,053
AFT BODY	1	55,192	8,491	55,237	8,498
OUTBOARD WING	2	7,495	1,153	7,540	1,160
CENTER WING	1	20,982	3,228	21,060	3,240
EXTERNAL	2	4,550	700	4,583	705

USABLE FUEL TOTALS

TANKS	POUNDS	GALLONS	NOTES
NO. 1, 2, 3 & 4 MAIN	152,204	23,416	Fully serviced quantities include both trapped and drainable fuel.
MAINS AND MID BODY	198,614	30,556	The tanks will have the quantities shown under conditions of ICAO standard day with fuel density of 6.5 pounds per gallon.
MAINS, MID BODY, FORWARD BODY & AFT BODY	267,125	41,096	See data supplied in Section V, "Operating Limitations" to determine fuel loading.
MAINS, ALL BODY, OUTBOARD WING & CENTER WING	303,097	46,630	
ALL TANKS	312,197	48,030	

NOTE: See data supplied in Section V, OPERATING LIMITATIONS to determine fuel loading.

External tanks have a slight nose up attitude when the aircraft is on the ground.

B-52G FUEL GRADE PROPERTIES & LIMITS

USE	FUEL TYPE	GRADE (In order of preference)	NATO SYMBOL	U.S. MILITARY SPECIFICATION	SPECIFIC GRAVITY (Max-Min at 60°F)	FREEZE POINT °F	LIMITS
RECOMMENDED FUEL	WIDE CUT GASOLINE	JP-4 [5]	F-40 ★	MIL-T-5624	.802-.751	-72	
ALTERNATE FUEL	WIDE CUT GASOLINE	COMMERCIAL JET B [5]	NONE	NONE	.802-.751	-56	[2]
	KEROSENE	JP-5	F-44	MIL-T-5624	.845-.788	-51	[1]
		COMMERCIAL JET A-1 [5]	F-34 ★	NONE	.829-.775	-54	[2][3]
		COMMERCIAL JET A [5]	NONE	NONE	.829-.775	-36	[2][3]
EMERGENCY FUEL	AVIATION GASOLINE (AVGAS) PLUS 3% MIL-L-22851 TYPE II	80/87	F-12	MIL-G-5572	.706 [4]	-76	[1]
		91/96	NONE	NONE	.709 [4]	-76	
		100/130	F-18	MIL-G-5572	.702 [4]	-76	
		108/135	NONE	NONE	.707 [4]	-76	
		115/145	F-22	MIL-G-5572	.706 [4]	-76	

★ Fuel identified by NATO symbols F-34 and F-40 contain a fuel system icing inhibitor.

[1] Follow climb restrictions.
[2] Avoid flying at altitudes where indicated OAT is below the freeze point of the fuel.
[3] Prior to using commercial fuel, obtain freeze point from vendor or airline supplying the fuel, then follow limit 2 above. The pilot should exercise caution if he suspects or observes improper fuel handling procedures. If there is any indication that cleanliness is not up to standard, a fuel sample should be taken in a glass container and observed for fogginess, presence of water or rust.
[4] Average value-limits are not controlled by specification.
[5] See figure 5-4, "Jet Fuel Mixture Freeze Point Charts."

Pre-camouflage view of the air refueling slipway and opened slipway doors.

Bomb doors are in three connected segments and are hydraulically operated by the left and right body hydraulic systems. An additional hinged section above the doors facilitates weapon loading.

Clip-in adapter rack is mounted in the ceiling of the forward portion of the bomb bay.

Three conventional cluster racks can be loaded. Each can carry 9 weapons for an internal total of 27.

Forward yoke assembly for CSRL (Common Strategic Rotary Launcher) installed in a B-52H. The CSRL fills the entire bay when loaded.

MHU-20/C CLIP-IN ASSEMBLY

ADU-13/C CLIP-IN ADAPTER & KMU-45/C MODIFICATION KIT

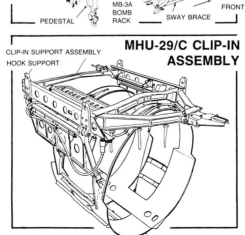

MHU-29/C CLIP-IN ASSEMBLY

BOMB LOADING CONFIGURATIONS HI-DENSITY

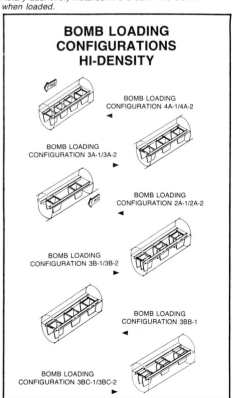

- BOMB LOADING CONFIGURATION 4A-1/4A-2
- BOMB LOADING CONFIGURATION 3A-1/3A-2
- BOMB LOADING CONFIGURATION 2A-1/2A-2
- BOMB LOADING CONFIGURATION 3B-1/3B-2
- BOMB LOADING CONFIGURATION 3BB-1
- BOMB LOADING CONFIGURATION 3BC-1/3BC-2

Aft yoke for CSRL. The CSRL itself weighs approximately 5,000 pounds and is compatible with B28, B61, or B83 bombs, and the AGM-86B and AGM-129 missiles.

CSRL power drive control unit. Launcher hydraulic power is normally from the #4 (left body) hydraulic system.

BC-1 BAY ASSEMBLY

1. BOMB RACK
2. TRANSVERSE BEAM
3. STOWAGE RECEPTACLES
4. CABLE CLAMP

CLUSTER RELEASE SEQUENCE

NORMAL RELEASE SEQUENCE

RAPID MINIMUM INTERVAL (RMI) RELEASE SEQUENCE

End view of bombs looking forward on aircraft incorporating T.O. 1B-52F-526 or 1B-52-1780

LOADING CONFIGURATION AND BOMB DROP SEQUENCE

END VIEW OF BOMBS LOOKING FORWARD

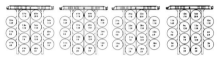

BOMB LOADING CONFIGURATION
4A-1 SEQUENCE DROP (56 BOMBS)

END VIEW OF BOMBS LOOKING FORWARD

BOMB LOADING CONFIGURATION
3A-1/3A-2 SEQUENCE DROP (42 BOMBS)

END VIEW OF BOMBS LOOKING FORWARD

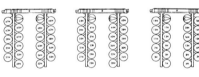

BOMB LOADING CONFIGURATION
BB-1 SEQUENCE DROP
D

END VIEW OF BOMBS LOOKING FORWARD

BOMB LOADING CONFIGURATION
3A-1 SEQUENCE DROP (36 BOMBS)
A

END VIEW OF BOMBS LOOKING FORWARD

BOMB LOADING CONFIGURATION
3B-1/3B-2 SEQUENCE DROP

END VIEW OF BOMBS LOOKING FORWARD

MINE LOADING CONFIGURATION
3BC-1 SEQUENCE DROP (18 MINES)

N-NORMAL RELEASE (Bombs released one at a time).
R-RAPID RELEASE (Bombs released three at a time with 3A and 3B bomb bay configuration of four at a time with 4A-1 bomb bay configuration).
A-Bomb sequence drop for M117R bombs only.
B-Uncocked A-6 releases (typical for all bays).
C-Cocked A-6 releases (unloaded).
D-Bomb sequence drop for Mk 82S bombs only.
E-A-6 must be cocked, but cannot be released BRIC pulses will be wasted whether or not A-6's are cocked. Stations with numbers will be cocked except 12, 24, and 36 BRIC pulse 37 single string initiation.

Munitions handling trailer carries a clip-in assembly holding four B28 bomb training "shapes". Clip-in racks are normally loaded in the forward bomb bay.

Four B61 bomb training shapes pre-loaded on a clip-in assembly. Hinged bomb doors facilitate positioning of the munitions handling trailer for loading.

Eight B83 training shapes loaded on a B-52H CSRL. The weapons are alternately staggered forward and aft.

B-52G, 58-0204, releases a B77 test round at the Sandia National Laboratories Tonopah Test Range. Smoke is from spin rockets used to stabilize the bomb's fall. President Carter cancelled B77.

McDonnell ADM-20C (then GAM-72) "Quail" decoy missile. Four "Quail" could be loaded in the bomb bay in addition to other clip-in weapons.

GAM-72 LAUNCHING SEQUENCE

NO. 4 MISSILE — NO. 2 MISSILE
NO. 3 MISSILE — NO. 1 MISSILE

1. BOMB BAY DOORS SWITCH - OPEN. THE LAUNCHING SEQUENCE IS BEGUN WHEN THE BOMB BAY DOORS SWITCH IS ACTUATED.

2. WHEN THE BOMB BAY DOORS ARE FULLY OPEN, AND THE MISSILE SELECTOR LAUNCH SWITCH IS ACTUATED, THE LOWER CARRIAGE WILL EXTEND THE NO. 1 (LEFT) MISSILE TO THE NO. 1 POSITION. MISSILE WINGS ARE SPREAD AND THE ENGINE IS STARTED AUTOMATICALLY. THE MISSILE IS LAUNCHED INTO FREE FLIGHT BY ACTUATION OF THE MISSILE LAUNCH SWITCH ON THE LAUNCH CONTROL PANEL.

3. ONCE THE MISSILE IS LAUNCHED, THE LOWER CARRIAGE IS JETTISONED AUTOMATICALLY.

4. THE UPPER (NO. 2) MISSILE CAN NOW BE SELECTED, EXTENDED AND LAUNCHED. AFTER THE UPPER MISSILE IS LAUNCHED, THE UPPER CARRIAGE RETRACTS, AND THE TRACKS FOLD AUTOMATICALLY.

5. THE LOWER (NO. 3) MISSILE IS EXTENDED, WINGS SPREAD, AND ENGINE STARTED. ONCE THE MISSILE IS LAUNCHED, THE LOWER CARRIAGE IS JETTISONED AUTOMATICALLY.

6. THE UPPER (NO. 4) MISSILE CAN NOW BE SELECTED, EXTENDED, AND LAUNCHED. AFTER THE UPPER MISSILE IS LAUNCHED, THE UPPER CARRIAGE RETRACTS, AND THE TRACKS FOLD AUTOMATICALLY.

7. LAUNCHING SEQUENCE COMPLETED. BOMB BAY DOORS CLOSED.

GAM72B STATIONS DIAGRAM

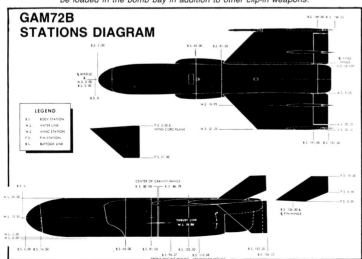

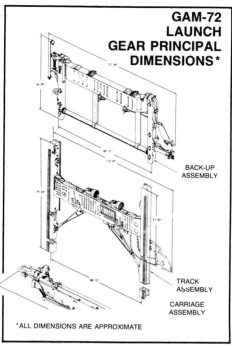

GAM-72 LAUNCH GEAR PRINCIPAL DIMENSIONS*

BACK-UP ASSEMBLY
TRACK ASSEMBLY
CARRIAGE ASSEMBLY

*ALL DIMENSIONS ARE APPROXIMATE

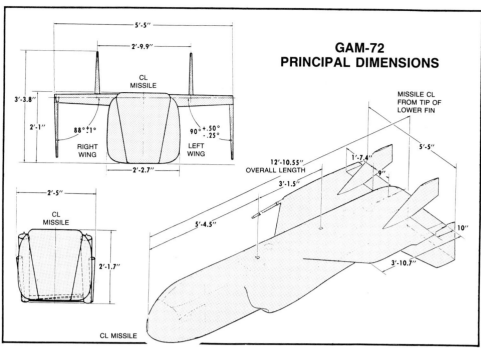

GAM-72 PRINCIPAL DIMENSIONS

GAM-72 MISSILE INTERIOR ARRANGEMENT

1. FORWARD BODY
FLIGHT CONTROL SYSTEM COMPONENTS
TRANSFER FUNCTION
AMPLIFIER
PROGRAMMER
SENSING INSTRUMENTS
GROUND CHECKOUT CONNECTOR
FORWARD BODY TERMINAL BLOCK
BAROMETRIC SWITCH
 OFFENSIVE SUBSYSTEM NO.2
 BREAKAWAY CONNECTOR SUPPORT
BRACKET
ANTI-START HOLDING DIODE
ANTI-START RELAY
ALTERNATOR DISCONNECT RELAY
THROTTLE CLOSE RELAY
JETTISON SAFETY RELAY
FCS CHECKOUT RELAY

FUNCTION SELECTOR RELAY
POWER SELECTOR RELAY
POWER SELECTOR REALY
BREAKAWAY CONNECTOR RECEPTACLE
MAIN POWER DISTRIBUTION BLOCK
ENGINE START TIME DELAY RELAY

2. AFT BODY AND ENGINE
AFT BODY TERMINAL BLOCK
FORWARD FUEL TANK
FUEL BOOST PUMP
BLEED AIR TURBINE ALTERNATOR
FUEL CONTROL
THROTTLE ACTUATOR
OIL TANK
ENGINE E.O. TANK
OFFENSIVE SUBSYSTEM NO. 3
AFT FUEL TANK

3. RIGHT WING
DESTRUCT JUMPER DISCONNECT
WINGSPREAD CONTROL RELAY
WINGSPREAD ACTUATOR RELAY
ENGINE COOL REALY
WINGFOLD ACTUATOR
ELEVON ACTUATOR
ELEVON
UPPER FIN
UPPER FIN FOLD MECHANISM
LOWER FINE
PITOT PROBE
PITOT HEATER RELAY

4. LEFT WING
RATE SWITCH
E.O. BOTTLE BLOCKING DIODE
FUEL SHUTOFF VALVE BLOCKING DIODE
WINGSPREAD MONITOR RELAY
WINGFOLD ACTUATOR RELAY
WINGFOLD ACTUATOR

ELEVON ACTUATOR
THROTTLES BYPASS RELAY
ELEVON
UPPER FIN
UPPER FIN FOLD MECHANISM
LOWER FIN

"Giant Fish" atmospheric sampling pod loaded on B-52H, 60-0052. Five ram air scoops intake air for particulate samplers inside the 2,000 lb. pod.

Ram air exhaust ports on the "Giant Fish" pod. The forward segment of the bomb doors are removed to load the pod. Control panels are at the gunner's seat.

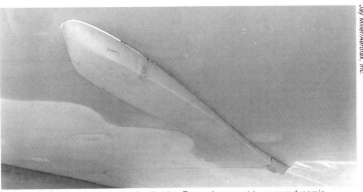
Fairing for external pylon hard point. Forward segment is an aerodynamic cover which is removed when a pylon is to be loaded.

Original "Hound Dog" pylon fairing was replaced with a wider, longer one on ALCM B-52G/H airplanes.

Stub pylon on "conventional" B-52G. I-beam adapter holds two Multiple Ejector Racks (MERs). Twelve weapons can be mounted in this configuration.

AGM-28 pylon with adapter beam and MERs is standard external conventional configuration on B-52H airplanes. Twelve Mk-82AIR bombs are loaded.

B-52G, 58-0237, at unstick with "Hound Dog" missiles loaded. The J52 engine on "Hound Dog" was started and the missile launched by the copilot.

EXTERNAL STORES CONFIGURATION

AGM-28 "Hound Dog" (62-0028) and pylon on handling trailer. Missiles were normally kept mated to their pylons and loaded to the B-52 as a unit.

AGM-28B, 62-0093, and pylon on handling trailer. "Hound Dog" fuselage contained fuel, navigational systems, and a W28 nuclear warhead.

GAM-87 "Skybolt" poses in front of JB-52H at Eglin AFB, Florida. "Skybolt", which had a solid-fuel propulsion system, was to have been a nuclear warhead-equipped ballistic missile with a range comparable to that of today's air-launched cruise missiles. Exhaust nozzle was faired-over with a disposable plastic cover.

Two "Skybolts" mounted under the left wing of a B-52G. Though the "Skybolt" was intended primarily for the H, some testing was done with the B-52G.

B-52H, 60-0062, was the test bed aircraft for the AGM-69A Short Range Attack Missile (SRAM). Aerodynamic fairings were installed on external SRAMs.

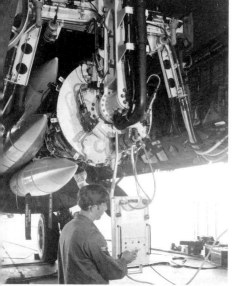
Munitions technician operates a ground-use control panel to rotate a SRAM rotary launcher.

SRAM external pylons utilized standard MAU-12 ejector racks for the AGM-69A missiles. Pylons contained missile interface units (MIUs) and environmental control systems.

AGM-69A ROTARY LAUNCHER & ADU-317/E ADAPTER

1. MISSILE LAUNCHER
2. ADU-317/E LAUNCHER-WEAPONS LOADER ADAPTER
3. SIGHT HOLE
4. QUICK-RELEASE PIN
5. ADJUSTMENT BOLT
6. BUMPER BLOCK
7. ADAPTER HOOK

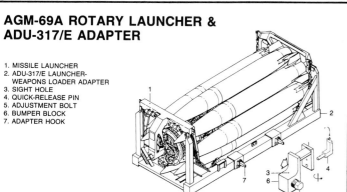

AGM-69A MISSILE ON TRAILER

1. MHU-69A/E MISSILE HANDLING CRADLES
2. CVU-112/E UMBILICAL RECEPTACLE PROTECTIVE COVER
3. MAU-12B/A EJECTOR
4. Deleted
5. MISSILE RESTRAINT FIXTURE RESTRAINT STRAPS
6. MMU-125/E MISSILE HANDLING FIXTURE
7. MHU-69A/E CRADLE RESTRAINT STRAPS
8. HANDLING FIXTURE AFT RESTRAINT STRAP
9. MHU-12/M MUNITIONS HANDLING TRAILER
10. REMOVABLE RAIL SECTION
11. TRAILER SPREADER BAR
12. MHU-71/E MISSILE HANDLING RAIL SET

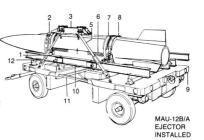
MAU-12B/A EJECTOR INSTALLED

AGM-86B ALCMs loaded into maintenace status on a B-52G. Restraints are installed on the flight control surfaces and pitot covers are installed. Note the aerodynamic "glove" on the pylon root.

The ALCM pylon weighs 4,450 pounds and supports six missiles with standard MAU-12 ejector racks.

General Dynamics AGM-109 "Tomahawk" ALCMs are posed with testbed B-52G, 58-0204. The losing ALCM entry, AGM-109 evolved into BGM-109 SLCM/GLCM.

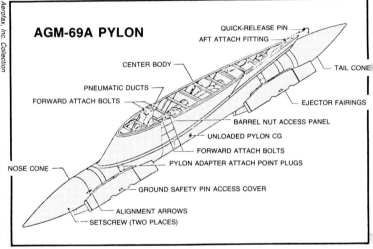

AGM-69A PYLON

- QUICK-RELEASE PIN
- AFT ATTACH FITTING
- CENTER BODY
- TAIL CONE
- PNEUMATIC DUCTS
- FORWARD ATTACH BOLTS
- EJECTOR FAIRINGS
- BARREL NUT ACCESS PANEL
- UNLOADED PYLON CG
- FORWARD ATTACH BOLTS
- NOSE CONE
- PYLON ADAPTER ATTACH POINT PLUGS
- GROUND SAFETY PIN ACCESS COVER
- ALIGNMENT ARROWS
- SETSCREW (TWO PLACES)

Mk 55 mine is one of a variety of mines compatible with the B-52G/H. Heavy mines such as this are loaded on clip-in racks and the HSAB.

Mk 52 mine is a 1,000 pound class mine that can be loaded internally on cluster racks (12 total) and externally on Heavy Stores Adapter Beams (HSABs).

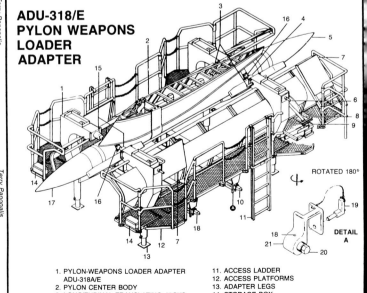

ADU-318/E PYLON WEAPONS LOADER ADAPTER

1. PYLON-WEAPONS LOADER ADAPTER ADU-318A/E
2. PYLON CENTER BODY
3. LONGITUDINAL TRANSLATING JACKS
4. AFT SUPPORT ARM
5. PYLON TAIL CONE
6. LATERAL DRIVE SCREWS
7. PLATFORM LEANING BOARDS
8. PITCH CONTROL DIAGONAL SUPPORT
9. BEAM ADAPTER
10. ADAPTER HOOKS
11. ACCESS LADDER
12. ACCESS PLATFORMS
13. ADAPTER LEGS
14. STORAGE BOX
15. FORWARD SUPPORT ARM
16. ADAPTER ATTACH BRACKET
17. PYLON NOSE CONE
18. SIGHT HOLE
19. QUICK-RELEASE PIN
20. ADJUSTMENT BOLT
21. BUMPER BLOCK

AGM-84 "Harpoon" antiship missiles loaded on B-52G, 58-0189, of the 320th BW. "Harpoon" is only carried externally on the Heavy Stores Adapter Beam (HSAB).

AGM-84 MISSILE IDENTIFICATION AND USAGE

DESIGNATION	NOMENCLATURE	USE	COLOR
AGM-84A-1, AGM-84C-1, AGM-84D-1	Surface Attack Guided Missille, Air	Tactical antiship weapon	White with yellow band around warhead section. Brown band around sustainer section
ATM-84A-1, ATM-84C-1, ATM-84D-1	Exercise Training Missile, Air	Training, test, and evaluation	White with blue band around exercise section. Brown band around sustainer section
ATM-84A-1B	Training Missile, Inert, Air	Handling, training	White with blue band around guidance section
ATM-84A-1C (Captive)	Ballistic Air Test Vehicle, Air	Handling, training captive carry	White with blue bands around the guidance, warhead, and sustainer sections
ATM-84A-1A, ATM-84C-1A, ATM-84D-1A	Training Missile, Inert Warhead, Air	Training, handling, and evaluation	White with blue band around inert warhead section. Brown band around sustainer section

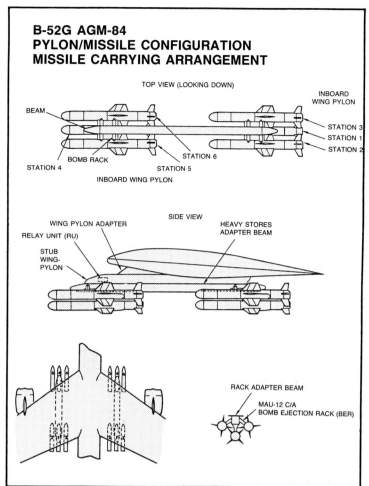

B-52G AGM-84 PYLON/MISSILE CONFIGURATION MISSILE CARRYING ARRANGEMENT

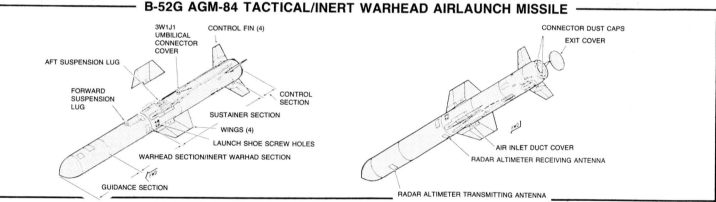

B-52G AGM-84 TACTICAL/INERT WARHEAD AIRLAUNCH MISSILE

Early configuration of B-52G tail armament featured an optical window for a television camera system, in space now occupied by ALQ-117 components.

ALQ-117 equipped B-52G. Turret has four M3s. ASG-15 search antenna is in the upper radome, while the track antenna is in the small radome between the guns.

B-52G turret modification is thought to be a heat pulse generating unit for infrared countermeasures.

B-52H features Emerson ASG-21 fire control system with dual search and track radars providing overlapping coverage aft. Protective "boot" covers M61 "Vulcan" gun mechanism.

Early configuration of B-52H, 60-0029. Aft fuselage is virtually devoid of ECM antennae.

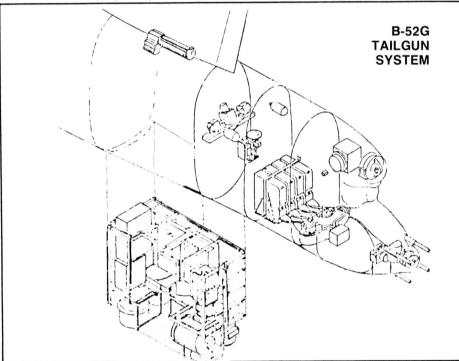

B-52G TAILGUN SYSTEM

Positioning of various ALQ-117 and RHAW antenna fairings around the B-52H FCS equipment.

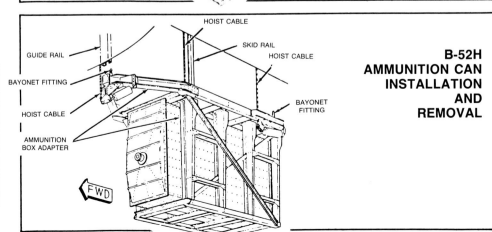

B-52H AMMUNITION CAN INSTALLATION AND REMOVAL

Access door for the 47 section is wired to the pilot's "Hatches Not Locked" caution indicator.

Lockheed D-21B drone is mated to B-52H external pylon for the first time on July 7, 1967 at the company's Burbank, California "Skunk Works" manufacturing facility.

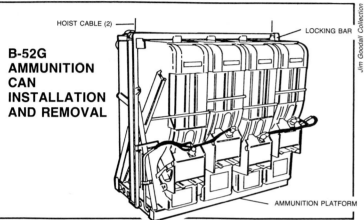

Jettisonable GTD-21B booster rocket unit was designed and manufactured by Lockheed specially for use in launching the drone from B-52H carrier aircraft.

Bomb bays of the D-21B carrier B-52H's were extensively modified to house support plumbing for the missiles. Date of photo May 22, 1967.

D-21B operation, support, and circuit breaker panels. Equipment is apparently mounted at the gunner's station.

Over the years since its inception a large number of upgrade studies have been proposed for the B-52. Two of the more recent include aircraft powered by turbofan engines in the 40,000 to 50,000 lb. thrust range. Any four of these engines would produce nearly twice the thrust of the B-52H's eight TF33s.

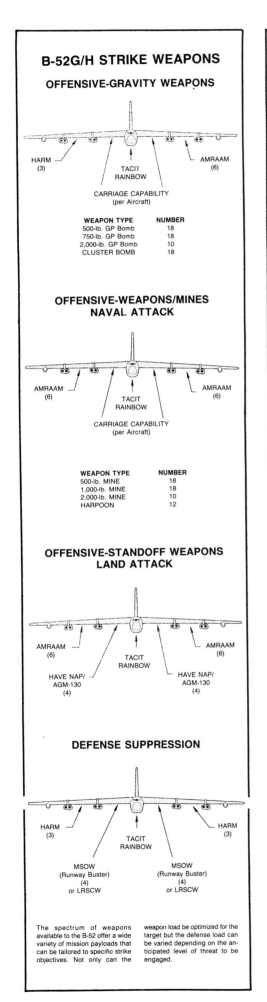
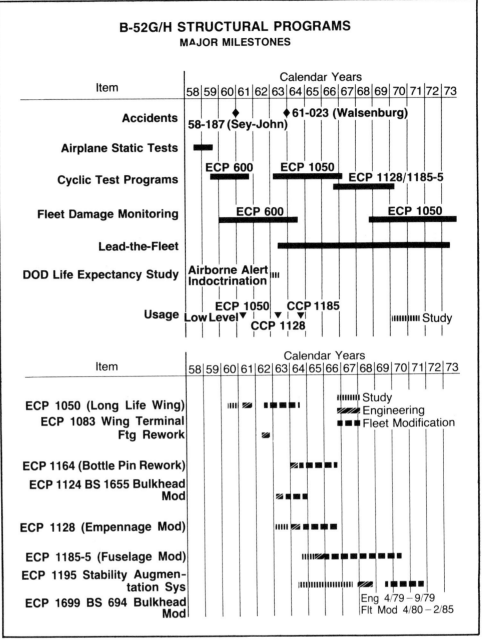
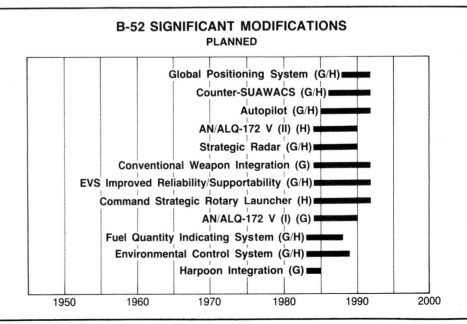